Betsy Brown ♡

The author with a group of hand puppets.

The hand puppets on the cover were photographed by Peter Croydon.

George Merten   **The hand puppets**

Publishers   Thomas Nelson and Sons

Toronto

New York

Edinburgh

Published simultaneously
in Canada and the United States

Library of Congress catalog
card number: 57 – 12752

The book was designed by
Frank Newfeld and
printed in Canada by
The Bryant Press Limited, Toronto.

Author's note

No book on puppetry can possibly begin to cover the field. Each separate phase would require volumes to itself. Nor is it desirable to give more than the basic requirements in any one area, or the essential creativeness of the medium is destroyed.

The purpose of this book is to give sufficient technical assistance regarding the construction of each of the puppet types dealt with to enable puppeteers to further their own techniques and exercise their imagination to the fullest extent.

Puppetry, like some other arts in these days, tends to become unnecessarily complicated in many of its uses. In this there is a danger that it may lose some of its charm, which lies largely in its simplicity, directness and illusion.

The use of puppetry in advertising, films and television is accepted as a part of progress, but it tends to introduce more and more 'gimmicks'. Too often these gimmicks replace artistry. Beware of the pitfall of relying almost entirely on such features as large staring eyes that roll around and other facial contortions of this nature to hold your show together. Although such practices are more common among users of marionettes, watch that the beautiful simplicity of a hand puppet, for instance, is not destroyed by such distractions. Limited facial animation, if well contrived and used sparingly, can be quite effective. Anything used too often soon loses its effectiveness.

We are none of us blameless in the field of over-animation and no doubt there are few who will avoid going through this phase. It may be a good thing to go through, but let it be a phase. Admittedly the working out of these movements has a certain fascination, but do not get so involved in the intricacies of the craft that the art is lost sight of. The element of surprise is essential, so be very selective in the use of these features.

A concentration on design and movement is much more rewarding and will hold the interest far longer. With increasing skill in modelling and with sensitive manipulation, a puppet's facial expression can appear to change without the necessity for built-in devices.

Never have there been so many puppeteers in the world as there are today, and their numbers are steadily increasing. It becomes even more important, therefore, to remember the long tradition of the puppet theatre which has through many centuries provided a variety of entertainment, based on illusion. This is a heritage we should be proud to carry on.

G. M.

Contents

An introduction to various types of puppet

Comparison cannot fairly be made between the relative merits of the various types of puppets. They are all necessary and legitimate, belong to the same medium and complement each other. Each type has advantages and disadvantages. The marionette can move in a wide area, sit down, kneel and in general do many things a live actor can do, besides a great many that the live actor cannot even attempt.

Marionette

The hand puppet is rather more limited in approximating human movement, but has perhaps on the whole better 'puppet' movement. The hand puppet can also make quicker and more sudden controlled movements than a marionette and can handle properties more easily than any other kind of puppet.

Hand Puppet

It is a very versatile creature and because the puppeteer is in direct contact with it he can control its movements to a fine degree.

It is also generally possible to have greater intimacy with the audience when using hand puppets, and they lend themselves readily to improvisations.

Intimacy

Hand puppets are relatively easy and quick to construct and simple to use, although it is very necessary to practise miming and to avoid just wagging the puppet about on the end of the hand. A great deal of subtlety can be attained by a hand puppet in the hands of a skilful manipulator.

Manipulation

The matter of legs on a hand puppet is largely an individual preference, although they are undoubtedly effective under certain circumstances.

Legs

Rods attached to the arms of a hand puppet give an opportunity for great expressiveness of movement, since the arms can be considerably longer. These puppets are particularly effective in very dramatic presentations, but have more limitations than the hand puppet in the handling of properties.

A purely rod puppet is also capable of beautiful and expressive movement. This type may have legs, or may have long clothing, as does a hand puppet. The puppet is controlled by various means, sometimes by external wires to the head and hands, and sometimes by a semi-mechanical method using a central wooden column running up through the puppet to which are attached levers and control wires. The operator holds the stick in one hand and operates with the other.

Another type of hand puppet is made by using a sock as the basis of the construction. This puppet usually has only a head, but the facial move-

1

ment that is possible with it makes it so effective that the lack of body parts is barely noticed.

Another directly controlled puppet is the finger puppet. This type uses the manipulator's fingers for legs. The arms may be made moveable by means of strings or constructed in a fixed position. It is a simple matter to make these figures move, but it takes considerable dexterity to make the most of their somewhat limited movement.

The shadow puppet is one of the oldest forms of puppetry and one which the Chinese carried to a very fine art. Shadows, like every type of puppet, can be extremely simple or highly intricate. One advantage in using shadows is that it is possible to show complete scenes and an illusion of depth in any amount of detail desired in a space about the same as that required for a hand puppet show. In addition, beautiful effects in the realms of fantasy are quite easily obtained, both in black and white and in colour.

Most types of puppets can be simplified to be suitable for use on playgrounds and in similar situations. Often one or another kind of paper or cardboard is used in their construction and, although these puppets may be less permanent, they serve their purpose very well indeed.

The unconventional

Do not be governed by the conventional. Make your puppets from any material that suggests itself to you. You must be right in your choice if it suits your purpose. There is no law which says a puppet shall be made of any particular material, or be of any particular shape, provided it is in character. Your own imagination is the yardstick. If it suits what you have in mind the head can be a pine cone, a door knob, a tin can, or shaped from a length of wire or piece of wood picked up in the forest. There is no other medium in the field of art that allows the artist as much licence as does puppetry. Take full advantage of this and do not stifle your creativeness.

The abstract and non-objective

'Abstract' is probably the most abused word in any art medium. It is more often than not confused with 'non-objective' and is applied to anything that is not understood. An abstraction should make sense because it is the essence of a logical thought.

A play can and should be to some extent abstract, but a play cannot be non-objective.

Abstraction, in the play sense, whether it is used to a greater or lesser degree, means that only the essentials are included, leaving a good deal to the imagination of the audience. Theatre may portray the everyday world or a world of fantasy, but in either case the difference between good and bad theatre is often what is omitted rather than what is included.

Exclude all but the essentials necessary to achieve the desired result, which, of course, should be clearly in mind at the outset. Let nothing stand in the way of the drama.

Abstraction is a form of simplification, another essential to good theatre. Eliminate all hazards. If a thing is too difficult, it is the wrong way and there is surely a better. Do not let a hazard jeopardize a whole show for a moment of possible effect. Remember that drama, not tricks, is the essence of theatre.

The hand puppet

The hand puppet

The basic part of the construction of a hand puppet is the glove or undergarment. If this is comfortable to wear it greatly assists the operation and general effectiveness of the puppet.

In the hands of a skilful and resourceful manipulator the head and hands of the puppet can be of the crudest, and yet the puppet lives. However, for general presentation it is desirable that a puppet should be well designed for the part it is to play. The design should be broad in treatment rather than detailed. This applies equally to the head as to the costume.

There are two distinct schools of thought as to which fingers of the hand should be used to operate the puppet. Some favour the thumb and the first two fingers to control the head and the arms, while others prefer to use the little finger instead of the second finger. Certainly the puppet looks better balanced using the latter method and is equally versatile. Probably it is a case of which method you begin with, although some feel that the little finger is not strong enough for the task of picking up properties and also lacks the capacity for movement. Experience proves, of course, that with practice the little finger becomes equally strong and versatile as the second finger and the puppet maintains a balanced look.

The method given here favours the use of the little finger, although either finger can be used according to preference.

The construction of the hands is directed to giving additional strength to whichever finger is used and also to giving extra length to the arms.

The undergarment assists in allowing the actual costume of the puppet to hang as effectively as possible by absorbing some of the unavoidable creasing caused by the movements of the manipulator's hand.

The general treatment of hand puppet construction is the same whether the puppets are humanized or animal characters, with the exception of large animals or reptiles that are built without front legs, such as alligators and dragons, when the whole hand is usually used to operate a moving mouth.

Construction

Materials

Cotton broadcloth

Stove pipe wire

White felt

Pair of cotton garden gloves

Needles and thread

Plasticine

Plaster of Paris

Plastic wood

Petroleum jelly

Glue

Tissue paper and two grades of building paper (for papier-mâché)

Cold water paste powder

Asbestos powder

French Chalk

Artist's oil colours:
Vermilion; Burnt Sienna; Scarlet Lake; Cobalt Blue; Mid Green; Yellow Ochre; Ivory Black; White

Soft hair brushes

Turpentine

Japan driers

Wool, theatrical crêpe hair, etc.

The head

It is useful to begin the construction of a hand puppet with the modelling and casting of the head, unless the head is already in existence. This procedure enables the costume and hands to be made during the various drying periods that are necessary before the head is complete and ready for attaching to the glove body.

Heads that are first modelled in plasticine and later taken from the moulds in either plastic wood or papier-mache, or when the papier-mache over-casting method is used, are described in detail. Some alternative methods of creating the puppet's head are given later.

An important part of the construction of a hand puppet head is the 'stopper' that is inserted in the neck to prevent the finger from going too far inside. The second joint of the finger acts as the puppet's neck joint, so if the joint is allowed to go in too far the finger will not bend and the movement of the head becomes very limited.

Anything that performs the function satisfactorily can be used as a stopper, such as building in a barrier of plastic wood or papier-mâché when the head is put together, but every consideration should be given to comfort and some padding may be necessary.

Simple, effective and comfortable stoppers can be made from the fingers of cheap cotton garden gloves that can be purchased from any dime store.

Modelling the head

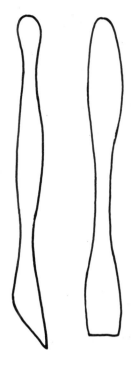

Model in clay or plasticine. Of the two mediums, plasticine is the cleaner and does not harden. In addition, it can be used over and over again.

If clay is used, the model must be kept covered with a damp cloth until the modelling and casting are completed. Clay is easier to remove from the plaster mould when damp.

For your general guidance a puppet head measuring approximately 4½ inches from the top of the head to the point of the chin will require about 2 lbs. of plasticine.

It is a good idea to measure out your material in this way because it is surprising how much the head tends to 'grow' in your hands as you model. Before long you realize it is larger than you meant it to be.

It is helpful to have one or two modelling tools. They can be purchased cheaply, but if you prefer to make your own, the shapes shown in the diagram will be found the most useful. See Fig. 1.

Head modelling is largely a matter of practice, but the following general procedure can be applied when beginning work on any head.

Do not try to build up a head feature by feature. 'Rough in' all the features of the face first and then continue to work on it as a whole.

Model about ⅔ of your plasticine into a rough ball shape. With the remainder you have to do further work on the head, model the features and make the neck.

With a wooden tool, or match stick, draw horizontal lines on your shape, as shown in photograph 1 on page 11. These lines indicate the positions of the eyebrows, the bottom of the nose and the mouth. The normal position of the eyes is approximately half-way between the top of the head and the chin, but certain liberties can be taken with the features generally, if desirable, when creating a puppet character.

Mark the width of the bridge of the nose and, with your modelling tool, cut out the eye sockets and the shape of the nose. The general form resulting is shown in photograph 2.

Having arrived at this basic form, the remainder of the modelling is largely that of giving to the head the character you have in mind. See photographs 3, 4, 5 and 6. The nose can be made larger or smaller, the eyes bulging or inset, the mouth serious or laughing.

A CLOWN may have a large nose, a domed head and a wide mouth. A NEGRO will have a profile slanting back from the chin to the forehead, a

Fig. 1

short broad nose and thick lips. An ORIENTAL will have slit eyes and high cheek-bones.

All the features must be somewhat exaggerated and, above all, treated broadly.

A bold treatment means that the character will 'carry' right to the back row of the audience. Too much detail in a face will confuse the character altogether.

To indicate cheerfulness the corners of the mouth should tend upwards. If the character is doleful the corners of the mouth should have a downward tendency.

The easiest way to form the eyes is to roll two small balls of plasticine and then place them in the eye sockets. Cut four short lengths of thinly rolled plasticine and press flat. Place two of·these in the position of the lower lids and then lay the other two pieces in the position of the upper lids and slightly overlapping the lower lids at the corners of the eyes. The upper lids should be slightly heavier than the lower. Use a tool to finish off the modelling.

Take care not to make your eyes too staring, but give them a 'quiet' look.

A thin application of petroleum jelly will assist in smoothing the head; be sure to use the least possible amount to achieve smoothness.

Ears may be modelled on the head if it helps you to get your effect. They may also be cast with the head, but removing them before casting saves an undercut. They are sometimes damaged when the head is taken from the mould, so it is quite a good idea to model them on at a later stage. The position of the ears in relation to the other features is shown in Fig. 2.

If preferred, the hair may be modelled on the head. Leave the neck fairly long; it can always be shortened later.

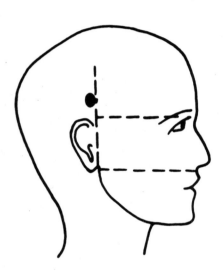

Fig. 2

* The sections under this heading are designed to assist puppeteers to avoid those pitfalls in construction that have been noted as most common in the author's experience. These hints have only been included where they are necessary or helpful.

The sections called 'Quick reference summary of method' are intended to save the puppeteer from constantly referring back in the text, particularly where the process is more involved, and also to ensure that the procedures are carried out in their right order.

Points to make and watch*

◎ Treat the features broadly. Do not confuse with small details that do not 'carry'.

◎ Make use of planes to create 'character shadows'.

◎ As a general rule, keep the eyes 'quiet'.

◎ Try to avoid modelling open mouths; they are apt to get monotonous.

◎ The neck should be modelled before the head is cast.

◎ Check that the eyes are looking straight ahead (not upwards) when the head is standing on the neck.

1   Indicate line of brow, bottom of nose and mouth (distance between mouth and nose is about half the length of the nose); indicate shape of nose.

2   Cut away, as shown, at position of eyes. (Cut from side, do not dig hole.)

A method of head modelling that easily establishes and maintains the proportions

3   Place in rough shapes at eyes, nose, lips and chin. At stages 3 and 4 the 'character' of the head should begin to develop.

4   Place in rough shapes for lower and upper lids, nostrils and cheeks. Use modelling tool on mouth and chin.

5   Do not ignore the profile when modelling the head. Keep turning the head about as the character is developed.

6   When 'roughing in' is completed use modelling tools to finish off the details.

Moulding the head

After modelling, puppet heads are moulded in plaster of Paris.

Preparing the plaster

7

Put about 2 pints of water in a medium sized bowl. Sift plaster into the water until it shows above the surface. This will be the approximate amount of plaster you will require, but be prepared to add a little more if it appears necessary. For use, the plaster should be the consistency of cream. Always add the plaster to the water, never add the water to the plaster. Make sure that there are no lumps in the plaster before applying it to the head. A good way to test the consistency is to draw one finger across the surface of the plaster. If a faint trace remains the plaster is ready to pour. (See photographs 7 and 8.)

Have the head prepared for moulding before mixing the plaster, otherwise the plaster may harden before you have time to use it. Preferably use an enamel or plastic bowl for mixing because it will clean more easily, even if surplus plaster has been allowed to dry.

8

Split head moulding for plastic wood heads

In preparation for the moulding the head is cut in half down through the centre of the face. Cutting it in this way will give you two equal and like halves and will eliminate most of the undercutting in a character head. This method also makes removal from the moulds easier. The moulds will also be shallower and the final castings will dry more quickly and evenly.

9

Take a piece of carpet thread or strong, fine wire and twist each end around a short stick. Use it like a cheese wire to cut the head in half (photograph 9).

It is easier to cut a plasticine head accurately if it is held by another person. When the head is held for cutting it should be taken between the palms of the hands with the features up and the neck towards the cutter. The thread should be laid along the length of the face. Take an end in each hand and, holding the end that goes over the top of the head, pull the other end carefully so that it cuts into the features. When the cut has been started, allow the string to touch, but not cross, under the head. Then pull on the end of the string that passes through the front of the face until the cutting is completed.

The main point here is that the wire or string must just touch under the head, but not cross; otherwise the cut will be uneven.

For the actual moulding, lay the two halves of the head on a flat surface, face to face, and place a shallow wooden frame around them, leaving a safe margin (photographs 10 and 11).

First apply the plaster by splashing it lightly onto the features until they are quite covered (photograph 12). Now gently 'puddle' the plaster into the features with the tips of the fingers, taking care not to damage them in any way. Complete the mould by pouring the remainder of the plaster carefully into the mould (photograph 13).

The average mould will be about three inches thick. Be sure that at the highest part, usually the side of the head, there is a covering of at least about ½" of plaster.

When the mould is dry enough, remove the plasticine with a screwdriver, or a piece of shaped wood, lifting from the back of the head (photograph 14). Do not use a modelling tool for this operation, because it may snap in half.

When the plasticine has been taken from the mould, break off any over-hang of plaster beyond the edge of the features. This is caused by some of the plaster running under the head during moulding. This often happens if the head has not been cut carefully. Now grease the inside of the mould thoroughly with paste floor wax and petroleum jelly.

Points to make and watch

◎ Lay the cutting string carefully down the centre of the face.

◎ The head must be held with the neck towards the person doing the cutting.

◎ Do not pull on both ends of the string simultaneously. Hold one end still and pull on the other.

◎ It is a good idea to stoop down when cutting through the head in order to watch the point at which the strings touch. This point must always remain in view and never be allowed to disappear inside the cut.

◎ The strings should just touch under the head, but *not cross*. The pulled string should ride lightly against the held string.

◎ Have a wooden frame ready. This can be used over and over again.

◎ Always have the head cut and in the frame before mixing the plaster.

◎ Always use an enamel or plastic bowl.

◎ Sift the plaster into the bowl with the hands, do not dump it in.

◎ Always add the plaster to the water; never pour the water on the plaster.

◎ Check that there are no lumps in the plaster before applying it to the head.

◎ Check that the features of the head are facing centre and about ½″ apart.

◎ Apply the plaster to the features first and then cover the head completely.

◎ 'Puddle' all round the edges of the head before building up the plaster to the correct thickness. Always keep the mould even and tidy.

◎ Always lift the plasticine from the back of the mould to prevent damage to features.

◎ Remove any overlapping plaster from the inside of the mould before greasing.

a   Cut the head carefully through the centre (photograph 9).

b   Lay the halves face to face in the wooden frame (photographs 10 and 11).

c   Mix the plaster (photographs 7 and 8).

d   Cover the features with plaster, then cover the rest of the head (photograph 12).

e   'Puddle' around the edges of each half to disperse air bubbles.

f   Pour the remaining plaster carefully over the head. Watch that the head doesn't move (photograph 13).

g   Check that the plaster is thick enough (if necessary more plaster can be added).

h   Allow the mould to dry thoroughly.

i   Turn the mould over and remove the frame.

j   Remove the plasticine from the mould (photograph 14).

k   Clean up the edges of the inside of the mould, but do not damage the features.

l   Grease the head thoroughly with paste floor wax and petroleum jelly. (Do not grease at this time unless the plastic wood is to be applied immediately.)

Making plastic wood heads

The plastic wood should be applied to the mould on an average of almost an eighth of an inch in thickness although it will be unavoidably thicker on parts of the features. The more uniform the thickness the less shrinkage. The average amount of shrinkage that does take place helps to make removal from the mould easier when it is thoroughly dry.

The wood must be left in the mould to dry naturally (36 to 48 hours). On no account should direct heat be applied although the mould can be left near a radiator.

Points to make and watch

◉ The mould must be thoroughly greased before the plastic wood is applied to it.

◉ The plastic wood should be less than an eighth of an inch thick and applied in as uniform thickness as possible.

◉ The mould can be left near a radiator to dry, but *no direct heat* should be applied.

◉ Test the dryness of the plastic wood before trying to remove from the mould by pressing at its thickest part. The amount of shrinkage is also an indication of how dry the wood is.

◉ When removing the two halves of the head from the mould, lift carefully from the back in order not to risk damage to the features.

◉ The head is now ready for joining together.

N.B. Plastic wood heads may be taken from either split or shim cast moulds, but mâché heads are best taken from shim cast moulds. This method of casting is described further on in the book.

Joining the head together

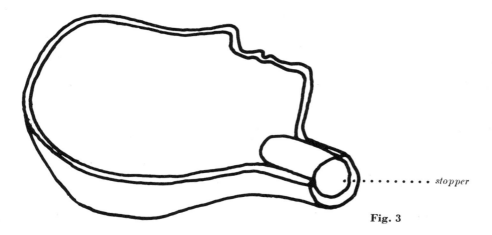

stopper

Fig. 3

Do not allow the halves of the head to stand too long after they have been taken from the mould before joining them together. If left too long they have a tendency to warp. Tools and materials needed:

◉ Sharp Knife / Glue / Plastic Wood / Vaseline / Glove finger

Should the halves have warped a little, or if the edges are very uneven, then the joining surfaces may be sanded with a circular motion on a piece of medium sandpaper lying flat on a table. This must be done judiciously and not made a general practice because, if overdone, the head can easily become too narrow.

Trim the edges of the two halves with a sharp knife and cut a small piece off the bottom of the neck. This allows for the insertion of the stopper (Fig. 3), which is part of a glove finger.

Glue around the edges and inside the neck on both halves of the head. Rub a little vaseline on the fingers to prevent the plastic wood from sticking. Place enough plastic wood in one side of the neck to cradle the stopper. Put a touch more glue on the plastic wood and set in the stopper.

Prepare the other side of the neck in the same way with plastic wood and glue. Then put a little plastic wood on top of the glue all around the edge of *one side of the head only.*

When this has been done place both sides together and carefully line up the features. If necessary the back of the head can be adjusted later.

Put the forefinger inside the stopper and ease it into a comfortable position. Then check that you are able to bend the second joint of the finger. If these precautions are not taken it may be found later, when the plastic wood is hard, that too much plastic wood was put in the neck, which would naturally affect the finger space. During the joining process the stopper could also have been accidentally pushed a little further into the neck and so most of the head movement would be lost.

The hand puppet

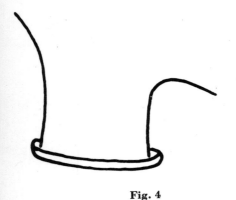

Fig. 4

Build a narrow rim around the bottom of the neck with plastic wood. See Fig. 4. When attaching the finished head to the costume the under glove is glued to the neck and pulled tight around it with a thread just above the rim. This makes it extremely unlikely that the head would ever come away from the body accidently.

Smooth the excess plastic wood into the join and set out to dry. The head must be left for some hours before further work on it is attempted.

Quick reference summary of method

a   Prepare and trim head for joining. Sand edges if necessary.

b   Cut finger from cotton glove.

c   Glue joining edges and inside of neck on both halves.

d   Rub a little vaseline on the hands.

e   Put plastic wood and glue on both halves of the neck.

f   Set the stopper in one side.

g   Put a little plastic wood all around the joining edge of *one side only*.

h   Press both sides together and line up the features.

i   Check width and position of stopper.

j   Smooth the excess plastic wood over the join.

k   Form a rim at the bottom of the neck with plastic wood.

l   Place head to dry. If it tends to spring apart, tie around with string.

Finishing plastic wood heads

Be certain that the join in the head is thoroughly dry and not likely to come apart when handled. Using a sharp knife and some medium sandpaper remove any ridge that may be noticeable at the join.

It will probably be necessary to fill in a little more at the join with plastic wood, particularly on the face. The plastic wood has a habit of sinking in along the join while the head is drying. Make good with plastic wood any other bad spots on the face. Any readjustment, or remodelling of the features should be done at this point, if such is desirable. The whole character can easily be altered using plastic wood as the modelling medium. Always remember to keep vaseline on the fingers when using plastic wood.

When all other adjustments have been made, the ears should be attached. Put a touch of glue on the head at the points where the ears are to be placed. Roll into a ball between the fingers sufficient plastic wood for one ear. Then roll it into a slightly elongated shape. Press between the thumb and forefinger and, using the other hand, form a rough kidney shape.

Check for size against the head. If the size is correct, place it on the spot of glue on the side of the head and spread the front of the ear with the thumb so that it joins smoothly into the head. Give the ear a little definition, using a modelling tool or suitable piece of wood.

When both ears are attached, leave to dry in a position that will not cause them damage while they are drying.

Points to make and watch

◎ The head must not be handled until the join is quite dry. This may only be a couple of hours or so, depending largely on the neatness of the work.

◎ Avoid pushing the stopper into the head. The neck takes longer to dry than the join.

◎ Fill in any remaining crack at the join.

◎ Carry out any adjustments, remodelling or patching up of rough spots.

◎ Glue the head ready for the ears.

◎ Vaseline the hands.

◎ Form the ears and check that they are not too large.

◎ Smear the ears to join smoothly with the rest of the head.

◎ Give some definition to the ears. This should not be overdone.

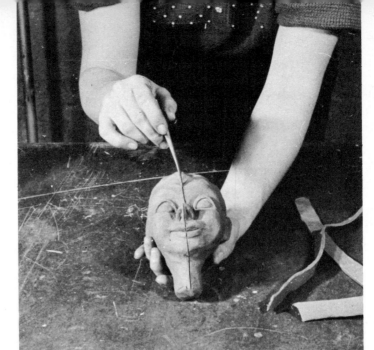

15

16

Shim casting

Moulds made by this method may be used for both plastic wood and papier-mâché heads. However, when making paper heads it is advisable to use the shim cast mould, because it is easier to match up the features since the head is turned out of the mould in one piece and warpage is practically eliminated.

Shims are anything which divide, and for this mould they can be either flat pieces of thin sheet metal, such as sheet tin or aluminum, or strips of plasticine, which are used in the method described here.

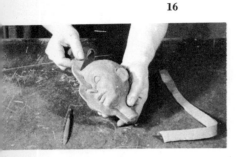

17

Divide your plasticine head by drawing a faint line running through the centre of the features from the neck to the top of the head, and then down the back of the head to the neck again (photograph 15).

Prepare strips of plasticine about ¾″ wide and not more than ⅛″ thick.

Starting at the neck, begin applying the plasticine strip at right angles to the line, following it exactly, but keeping it visible. Continue up over the features, taking great care not to destroy or distort them. End this strip at the top of the head.

18

Press the plasticine strip against the head just enough to be sure that it is firm and there is no gap through which the plaster could run (photograph 16).

Starting from the top, run another strip down the back of the head in exactly the same manner as before. Press the join at the top firmly together.

Now take a short strip of plasticine and lay it around the bottom of the neck at right angles to the neck, from one divider to the other. Make sure that the original dividing line is on this side (photograph 17).

Lay the head carefully on its side in a 'nest' of soft paper, taking care that the side with the collar on the neck is uppermost.

19

Take another strip of plasticine and run it from the collar on the edge of the neck right around the dividing strip back to the neck on the other side (photograph 18). This creates a wall that will contain the plaster and prevent it from running away.

Mix two to three cups of plaster in the same way as for other types of mould making (see page 18). Pour slowly over the head. Any air bubbles that begin to form can be quickly dispersed by using a finger and 'puddling' the plaster (photograph 19).

20

Gradually build up the same thickness of plaster over the whole head to the thickness of the dividing wall.

Now build up the plaster at the top of the mould over the ear and, using a wet knife, flatten the surface in order that a substantial base is formed on which to stand the mould (photograph 20).

Let this half of the mould set.

21

When it is dry turn the mould over and remove the plasticine dividers.

Using a pointed knife gently scrape the ¾-inch plaster margin until flat and smooth, taking care that the inside edge is not chipped or the features damaged (photograph 21).

With the point of the knife dig three equally spaced holes, about ½ inch deep, in the centre of the margin.

Grease the margin and the lug holes thoroughly with petroleum jelly.

Put a collar on the bottom of the neck in the same way as for the first half of the mould (photograph 22).

22

Mix some more plaster in the bowl.

Pour the plaster over the head in the same way as previously and scrape clean where it runs over the seam of the first part of the mould so that you have a similar edge as before and the dividing crack is clearly visible (photograph 23).

Let the plaster dry thoroughly.

23

When it is dry tap the mould gently in a number of places around the crack and lever the two halves apart (photograph 24).

Remove the plasticine from the mould.

If any air holes are visible, use a small quantity of plaster to patch them after first putting a drop of water in the hole.

Smooth the patch with a wet finger.

21

24

Points to make and watch

◎ In general plasticine dividers are the simplest for beginners.

◎ Draw the guide line on the head as accurately as possible.

◎ Take care that the plasticine dividing strips are prepared in close conformity to the suggested measurements.

◎ If metal shims are used, cut the pieces to a size of about 1″ x 1½″ and stick them into the head along the guide line, overlapping each piece slightly so as not to leave any gaps.

◎ Start applying the dividing strips at the neck.

◎ Press the plasticine strips close to the head to close any gaps, but do not disturb the features.

◎ Remember to make a collar at the bottom of the neck and to cast with this uppermost.

◎ Remember to build the strip that is attached to the dividing strip that forms a 'wall' for the mould, otherwise the plaster will run off the head during casting. A plasticine 'wall' should also be placed around metal shims.

◎ Check the method of mixing the plaster and mix enough for one half of the mould only. See page 18.

◎ Build up an adequate thickness of plaster over the head and use a wet knife to shape the mould and flatten the top.

◎ Take care that the holes for the lugs are made deep enough and are correctly spaced.

◎ Grease the edge of the mould thoroughly, including the lug holes. The lugs are formed, of course, when the other half of the mould is made and plaster fills the holes.

◎ Place another collar around the neck before making the second half of the mould.

◎ Remember to scrape the overflow plaster clear of the seam between the two halves. Separate them when they are quite dry. It is better to scrape along the seam when the plaster is still damp.

Quick reference summary of method

a Draw the guide line for the dividing of the head with the plasticine strips (photograph 15).

b Prepare the plasticine strips ⅛″ x ¾″.

c Start at the neck and apply the strips up over the face. Do not cover the line (photograph 16).

d Carry the strip to the top of the head.

e Place strip down the back of the head.

f Lay the collar around half the neck on the side of the head where the dividing line shows (photograph 17).

g Make the 'nest' of soft paper and lay the head on it with the collar uppermost.

h Attach the plasticine wall to the dividing strip (photograph 18).

i Mix some plaster.

j Pour or spoon the plaster onto the head (photograph 19).

k Use a wet knife to shape the plaster and flatten the top of the mould (photograph 20).

l Let the plaster set hard.

m Turn the mould over and remove the divider, collar and wall.

n Gently scrape the plaster margin until it is flat and smooth (photograph 21).

o Hollow out the lug holes with the point of a knife.

p Grease the plaster margin and lug holes thoroughly.

q Put a collar around the bottom of the neck (photograph 22).

r Mix some more plaster.

s Pour or spoon the plaster onto the head.

t While the plaster is still damp, scrape excess away from the seam (photograph 23).

u Let the mould dry thoroughly.

v Tap the mould gently around seam and open (photograph 24).

w Remove the plasticine.

x Patch the mould if required.

Casting heads in papier-mâché

The use of papier-mâché is certainly the cheapest way to make a puppet head. There are two principal ways of making mâché heads. One is to overcast the modelled head with paper, which will be described later. The other method is to cast the whole head from a plaster mould.

For this method use the shim cast mould just described. Shellac the mould and allow it to dry thoroughly.

The following materials should be on hand to cast in papier-mâché:
Grey building, or roofing paper (available at most hardwares).
A heavier building paper, or heavy shipping paper.
Cold water paste powder.
Sharp pointed knife.
1″ paint brush.
Wooden tool, rounded at one end.
1 bowl.

Tear both grades of the grey building paper into strips roughly 3″ x 12″. Tear off all factory cut edges.

Pass the paper strips quickly through clean water and put the two grades in separate piles.

Mix the cold water paste in the bowl.

Using the lighter paper first, paste the top side only.

Tear the paper into smaller strips about 1″ wide and lay in one half of the mould, with the *pasted side up*, starting at the back of the head. Allow the paper to overlap the sides about 1″ all the way round (photograph 25).

Make certain the paper lies perfectly flat without creases or bubbles. The paper should be torn as necessary to form overlaps in order that it will lie flat more easily.

Continue laying in strips of paper across the head, finishing with the features.

Each piece of paper should overlap slightly, but not too much as this would tend to make the head vary in thickness.

It will be found easier to use smaller pieces of paper when covering the features.

Press the paper well into the features in order not to lose the original definition.

25

When the inside of the head is quite covered, give it a thin coat of paste.

Now take strips of the heavier grade of paper and paste both sides.

Narrow down the paper by tearing and apply to the mould in exactly the same way as before, but *do not overlap* the edge.

Now take the other half of the mould and lay the paper in it in exactly the same way as for the first half, but *overlap* both grades of paper.

26

When both halves have been papered, carefully lift each of the paper casts from the moulds and then push them gently back into place again. This is done to prevent the possibility of the casts sticking to the moulds in the event that some of the paste had accidentally been put on the plaster, or had saturated through the paper.

27

Take the half with the double overlap and tear the edge of the paper in to the edge of the mould as necessary to enable the paper to be folded across toward the centre of the mould. Do not turn the paper down inside the mould (photograph 26).

Now place this half mould carefully on top of the other half, matching the pegs to the notches on the mould (photograph 27). Hold the halves firmly together and run a finger around the inside of the neck, pressing the overlapping paper firmly over the seam between the two halves. Work with the finger as far into the head as possible, but take care not to disturb the set of the mould.

28

To complete the overlapping of the seam, reach inside the head with the rounded wooden tool and press down the remainder of the overlap firmly over the seam. Still holding the mould together, paste an additional layer of the heavier paper inside the neck. This will give it good reinforcement (photograph 28).

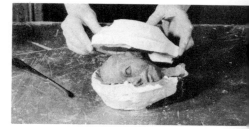

29

Carefully remove the top half of the mould and paint a thin coat of paste over the exposed half of the head (photograph 29). This ensures that all the edges are well pasted down.

Tear the outside overlap at intervals to within a ¼″ of the head and, using the pointed knife, lift and paste the overlapping pieces to the head, taking particular care with respect to the features (photograph 30). The sealing of the two halves is now complete. Allow the exposed part of the head to dry in the half mould until it holds its shape.

Remove the head completely from the mould and paste the lower half.

Rest the head on the drier side and allow to dry thoroughly all over.

30

When the head is quite dry sand it where necessary. After sanding give the head another complete pasting and let it dry again. This final pasting eliminates the slight 'fuzziness' resulting from the sanding.

Glue a piece of soft wood firmly into the neck opening. This will then give the same result as in the plastic wood heads.

Points to make and watch

◉ Use the shim method for making the mould for mâché heads.

◉ Remember to shellac the mould. Do *not* grease it.

◉ Tear off all factory cut edges on all the paper used.

◉ Do not soak the building paper for a long period.

◉ Be sure to make the paste thick enough.

◉ Remember that the first layer of building paper is pasted on one side only.

◉ The paper must be laid in the mould with the pasted side uppermost.

◉ Start laying the paper in from the back of the head and work towards the features.

◉ Tear the paper as necessary to form small overlaps so that it lies perfectly flat.

◉ Remember that the *first layer* of paper overlaps the edge all the way around.

◉ Use smaller pieces of paper on the features and press well into the definition.

◉ Do not let the pieces, or strips of paper, overlap each other more than is absolutely necessary.

◉ Paste both sides of the second layer of paper, but *do not overlap* edges.

◉ When lining the second half of the mould, carry out exactly the same procedure, but overlap both grades of paper.

◉ Remember to ease both halves of the head in the moulds before placing one mould on top of the other.

◉ Remember to fold the overlapping paper of the second half of the mould (double overlap) across towards the centre. Do not turn it down inside the mould.

◉ Always place the second half of the mould on top of the first half, not vice versa.

◉ Take care to match the lugs to the correct holes.

◉ Remember to use the finger as far up as possible through the neck hole to press the overlap down over the join.

◉ Take care not to disturb the set of the mould when doing this.

◉ Have the wooden tool ready to complete the overlapping.

◉ Remember to reinforce the inside of the neck.

◉ Do not damage the features when removing the top of the mould, or when turning up the outside overlap.

◉ Make sure the head is thoroughly dry before giving it too much handling.

a　Shellac the shim cast mould.

b　Tear both grades of building paper to the suggested size. Tear all factory cut edges.

c　Pass the paper through water.

d　Mix the cold water paste.

e　Paste the lighter grade of paper on one side only.

f　Tear the paper into narrower strips and begin laying in the mould, starting at the back of the head (photograph 25). Allow the paper to overlap about 1″ all round the edge.

g　Lay smaller pieces in the features.

h　Apply a thin coat of paste to the head.

i　Paste *both sides* of the heavier grade of paper.

j　Tear the paper into narrower strips and apply as before, but do not overlap the edge.

k　Lay in both grades of paper in the same way as for the first half of the mould, but allow both layers to overlap the edge.

l　Gently ease both halves of the paper head in the mould and then push them lightly back into place.

m　Take the second half of the mould and tear the overlapping paper to the edge of the mould and fold it in towards the centre (photograph 26).

n　Place this half of the mould on top of the other half (photograph 27).

o　Insert a finger in the neck and press the overlap over the seam.

p　Finish the overlapping with the wooden tool (photograph 28).

q　Paste extra paper inside the neck.

r　Remove the top half of the mould (photograph 29).

s　Give the half of the head that now shows a thin coat of paste.

t　Tear the outside overlap close to the head and lift up over the outside seam with a small knife (photograph 30).

u　Dry the exposed part of the head until it holds its shape.

v　Remove the entire head from the mould and paste the other half.

w　Dry the head thoroughly while resting on the drier half.

x　Sand as necessary and paste whole head again.

y　Glue a piece of soft wood firmly in the neck opening.

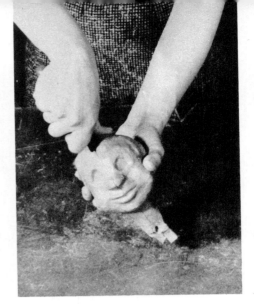

31   32

Overcast papier-mâché method

This is a simple way to make a papier-mâché head without having to make a plaster mould first. This method will be found particularly useful in schools, hospitals and libraries.

When overcasting a head the features should be very clearly defined when they are modelled, because there is some slight loss of definition during the casting process.

Drive a fairly large nail through a square of wood so that the nail sticks through an inch or so. Stand the head up on this nail. This will make the head easy to handle during casting.

Dip small pieces of tissue paper, preferably brown, in some water and cover the head with them as smoothly as possible.

Take strips of both grades of the grey building papers as used in the casting from the mould method mentioned earlier, and wet them thoroughly.

Paste the heavier grade of paper on one side only and lay on the head with the pasted side up (photograph 31). Again use small pieces on the features and press them well into the definition.

In all cases do not overlap each piece more than is absolutely necessary.

When the head is completely covered start again, using the lighter building paper, which should be pasted on both sides.

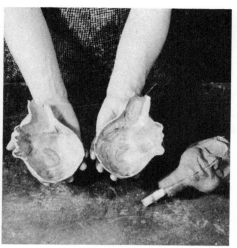

33   34   35

When this covering is completed, paste the head all over.

Now paste on another layer of the tissue paper, using as large pieces as practical in order to give the smoothest possible finish.

Allow the head to dry.

When thoroughly dry, use a sharp, thin-bladed knife, or razor blade in a holder, and cut through the cast into the plasticine, either down the centre of the face or across the head through the ears, according to the complexity of the features (photograph 32).

Remove the two halves of the paper head from the plasticine (photographs 33 and 34).

Fasten the two halves together again *immediately*, to prevent them from warping. This can be done with either scotch tape or a clamp-gun stapler (photograph 35).

Seal the cut edge by pasting narrow strips of ordinary thin brown paper over it. Let the head dry again.

If necessary sharpen or restore any part of the features, using the modelling composition described on page 38.

First sand and then paste the head and then paint it with flat white before giving it the final painting.

The hand puppet

Points to make and watch

◎ Tend to over-emphasize the definition when modelling a head for over-casting in order to compensate for the slight loss of definition during the casting process.

◎ Wet, but do not paste, the first layer of tissue paper.

◎ Wet both grades of building paper, but paste the heavier grade (which is applied first) *on one side only* and apply to the head with the pasted side uppermost.

◎ Paste the second layer of building paper on both sides.

◎ Use small pieces of paper, particularly on the features.

◎ Overlap the pieces of paper as little as possible.

◎ Do not use any 'cut' edges of paper, but tear all edges.

◎ When covering the head with the final layer of tissue paper, use as large pieces as practical in order to cover the joins in the heavier paper and leave the total surface as smooth as possible.

◎ Do not attempt to cut the paper from the plasticine head until all the layers of paper are *completely dry*.

◎ Remember to join the two halves of the head together again *immediately* after removing them from the plasticine.

◎ Do not use scotch tape over the complete join, only use three or **four** small pieces at intervals.

◎ Seal the entire join with small pieces of well-pasted ordinary brown wrapping paper.

a   Model a plasticine head with well-defined features.

b   Place the head upright on the nail through the board.

c   Tear the brown tissue paper into strips and pass quickly through water.

d   Apply pieces of the brown tissue paper to the head.

e   Tear enough of both grades of the building paper into strips and soak in water for a few seconds.

f   Paste the heavier paper *on one side only* and apply to the head with the pasted side uppermost. Press the paper well into the definition. A modelling tool is useful here. Use small pieces of paper on the features (photograph 31).

g   Paste the lighter grade of paper on *both sides* and apply to the head in exactly the same way as the heavier paper.

h   Cover the head with large pieces of the brown tissue paper, laid on as smoothly as possible, and paste thoroughly.

i   Allow the head to dry completely. Some heat can be applied, but care must be taken to prevent the plasticine getting too soft as the oil may penetrate through the paper.

j   Draw a line round the head where it is to be cut.

k   Use a sharp razor blade in a holder, or an X-acto knife, and cut right through the paper. Do not worry if the inside layer of tissue paper peels away in places (photograph 32).

l   Carefully remove the two sides of the paper head from the plasticine (photographs 33 and 34).

m   Join the two halves together, using a clamp-gun stapler at the neck and two or three small pieces of scotch tape at intervals around the head. Do not cover the complete join with scotch tape (photograph 35). (If no stapler is available, use a little scotch tape at the neck also.)

n   Paste small pieces of brown wrapping paper over the entire join.

o   Allow the head to dry thoroughly.

36

37

Finishing papier-mâché heads

A useful modelling composition

Should it be necessary to restore or sharpen the features on a papier-mâché head, the following composition will be found very useful. This compound should not be used on plastic wood heads.

Mix a small quantity of cold water paste and add some dry asbestos powder, mixing it into a moist dough. To this add sufficient French chalk (No. 1 talcum powder) until the dough is dry enough not to stick to the fingers. Apply the composition to the head as required and model, smoothing the work with the blade of a small knife frequently dipped in water (photographs 36 and 37).

After the modelling is completed, allow to dry and then sand.

Finishing coat for papier-mâché

38

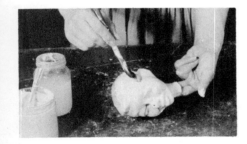

Mix some cold water paste as before. Add French chalk slowly, *beating very thoroughly*, until the mixture stands in peaks. Paint the head completely with the mixture, giving it as even a coat as possible (photograph 38). Smooth out by using a soft, flat paint brush dipped frequently into water (photograph 39). Be careful to smooth it out, not spread it out.

Allow to dry. If cracks appear when it is dry, the mixture was either too thin or unevenly applied. Sand with a fine-grain sandpaper until the surface is as smooth as required. Paste the head once again and let it dry. Give the head a coat of flat white paint before painting it in the usual manner.

39

String positions on a papier-mâché head

Due to the thin construction of papier-mâché heads it is not practical to use screw eyes unless the points at which they are placed are reinforced.

A satisfactory method of obtaining strong positions for the strings is to complete the head and, when the exact position of the strings has been ascertained, make a small hole on either side with a fine awl. Push a piece of stove pipe wire through the holes and allow about three-quarters of an inch to stick out on either side of the head. Using a pair of pointed-nosed pliers, roll these ends into loops close to the sides of the head.

Celastic method

'Celastic' is the trade name of a material used quite widely in the United States, not only for puppet heads, but for puppet bodies and properties as well. It is purchased by the yard and is rather more expensive than plastic wood and much more so than papier-mâché.

In addition to the Celastic material it is necessary to buy the 'parting agent', which prevents the Celastic from sticking to the mould, and some acetone.

The mould should be wetted before using Celastic.

Next the mould should be brushed over with the parting agent.

The Celastic should be torn into strips and made pliable with the acetone.

The Celastic is laid in the mould in much the same way as when using the papier-mâché method.

Keep the Celastic nicely moist, but not too wet.

Press well into the mould.

Two layers are usually sufficient.

When dry, remove from the mould and, if there is more than one section, join them together with strips of Celastic.

Celastic is light and strong to the point of being practically unbreakable. It can be sanded easily and takes paint well.

When using Celastic always work in a well-ventilated room as the fumes can be unpleasant. Rubber gloves would give added protection.

Layers of Celastic may also be used to reinforce a thinly made plastic wood head. The usefulness here being that it adds strength without adding weight.

Puppet bodies made of this material will have to be studied for balance. It will probably be necessary to compensate for lack of weight.

Large properties can be modelled in plasticine or clay and covered with Celastic. When dry the Celastic is cut off and the halves joined together again, using further strips of the material.

The same process with regard to properties can also be carried out, using the papier-mâché overcast method described earlier in this book.

Painting the head

If possible use oil colours when painting puppet heads. Oils are more durable than water paints. The faces can be cleaned by lightly washing them with a weak solution of ammonia and water if they get a little dirty.

The following colours will be found adequate for general painting: Vermilion, Burnt Sienna, Scarlet Lake, Cobalt Blue, Yellow Ochre, Black, and White.

Paint the whole head at one sitting. This enables you to work up better skin textures and to grade your colours more effectively.

A good basic flesh colour can be made with White, Yellow Ochre and a touch of Vermilion. If you wish to make the complexion more sallow add a little Blue. To tan the skin add a little Burnt Sienna. Do not paint the lips of men puppets a bright red, but add a little red to the flesh colour.

Only general hints on painting are possible here because it will be found that each head needs individual treatment. It will help considerably to make your painting effective if most of the character is 'built in' when the head is modelled and not left to be painted on. By doing this you obtain natural shadows which merely need accentuation with colour. Remember that bright stage lights will tend to lighten your colours, so make them fairly strong.

Points to make and watch

⊚ A shadow on the eyelids is effective for stage use. The colour of the shadow will vary, but generally will be grey, blue-grey, a shade of mauve, green or blue-green. Do not apply the shadow too heavily.

⊚ A fleck of white on the pupil of the finished eye gives it 'life'.

⊚ Do not paint the lips of male puppets a bright red, but mix a little more red with the flesh colour.

⊚ The lips of female puppets are made more effective if they are brushed over with clear lacquer, or nail varnish, when the paint is quite dry.

⊚ The eyes of all puppets can be treated with varnish or lacquer when dry.

⊚ The painting of the head should be completed at one sitting. This enables the working-up of better skin textures and grades the colours more effectively.

⊚ Stage lighting will tend to lighten the colours, so make them fairly strong.

⊚ Do not varnish puppet heads; they will reflect light and lose definition.

34

Wigging the head

The painting should be completed and the head quite dry before wigging.

Hair may be modelled on with papier-mâché or plastic wood and then painted. Other materials that are suitable for wigging are wool, frayed-out rope, embroidery silk, string, crêpe or real hair.

Crêpe hair is very frizzy when bought. It can be straightened by dampening with water and hanging up to dry with a weight attached.

Points to make and watch

◎ Before wigging, the head should be propped upright, or held by the neck in a vise.

◎ Glue the part of the head to be covered. Using a few strands at a time, work up and over from the back, finishing at the forehead. Leave the hair longer than necessary and trim after the glue has thoroughly dried.

◎ Plenty of hair should be put on because a certain amount will come out in the final dressing.

◎ Take trouble with wigging because a shabby hair-do can as easily spoil the appearance of a good puppet as it can that of a human being.

Some other methods of making the head

Basic round head design

This system enables a number of basic round head shapes to be stockpiled and completed later according to need and the character required.

Make a ball, or slightly elliptical shape, with plasticine and add the neck. Use one of the plaster moulding methods given earlier, according to whether the head will be finally cast in plastic wood or papier-mâché.

Complete the operation, including the joining of the head, if made of plastic wood. Insert the neck stopper and add the rim at the base of the neck.

If desired the features can be merely painted on the head, but with little extra time and trouble a great deal more character can be given by modelling at least some of the features, using either plastic wood or the modelling compound used to build up on papier-mâché heads. Usually it is sufficient to model only the nose and the ears, while the eyes and mouth are painted. An amazing number of character types is possible using this simple means, as will be seen from some of the puppet characters in the Photofolio section.

Wool, fur and a number of other materials make good hair.

Single round heads can also be made by using the overcast papier-mâché method.

Rubber ball head

Take a rubber ball of the approximate size of the desired head. Make a hole in it large enough to insert the forefinger, but only up to the second joint. The rubber should grip the finger at that point and so make the usual stopper unnecessary. The features can either be glued or just painted on this type of head. Rubber-based paint is recommended for this purpose. With this type the head will tend to sit on the shoulders since there is no neck. If desirable a neck can be contrived by forming a short tube of cardboard, to which the costume is glued. In this case it is not absolutely necessary to attach the head to the neck as the grip of the rubber will hardly allow it to fall off. This method also facilitates the use of differently costumed gloves for the same character.

Cloth heads

Effective hand puppet heads can be made from cloth, or an old stocking, stuffed with kapok. The features can be appliquéd on to the head. The nose, for instance, could be a small, shaped, kapok-filled bag. The eyes could be buttons, or felt, with felt eyelids. The ears and mouth could also be of felt, or any other material that suggests itself.

These heads may be painted, preferably using a water paint, or a flesh-coloured material could be used in the construction and the features left in their own colours. Wool or fur makes effective hair.

Felt heads

Felt heads are best constructed by sewing panels of felt to form the required shapes, leaving a hole for the neck. The neck can be made from a roll of cardboard covered with felt. In all cases remember that a 'stopper' should be inserted in the neck to obtain the maximum of head movement. (There is an exception to this rule, which will be dealt with later.) The features for these heads can be of similar materials to those suggested for cloth heads. The heads do not require painting as the felt colours should be chosen for their suitability in this respect.

Balsa wood heads

Because balsa wood is so soft and without a difficult grain, it is very easy to carve with a sharp knife. Start with a block of balsa wood that is larger than the required head and long enough to include the neck. Hobby shops usually carry balsa wood of a sufficient size for this purpose.

Sketch the profile on one side of the block and cut away the excess wood. This leaves a square face, but it can soon be given shape by rounding off the corners and modulating the features until the desired expression is obtained.

Before taking too much wood off the head, draw in the mass of the ears on the front of the head and cut around them when working on the features, until the time comes to shape them also.

Remember always to use a larger block of wood than the required head and always exaggerate the features when drawing the profile. It is easier, in this case, to take away than to add.

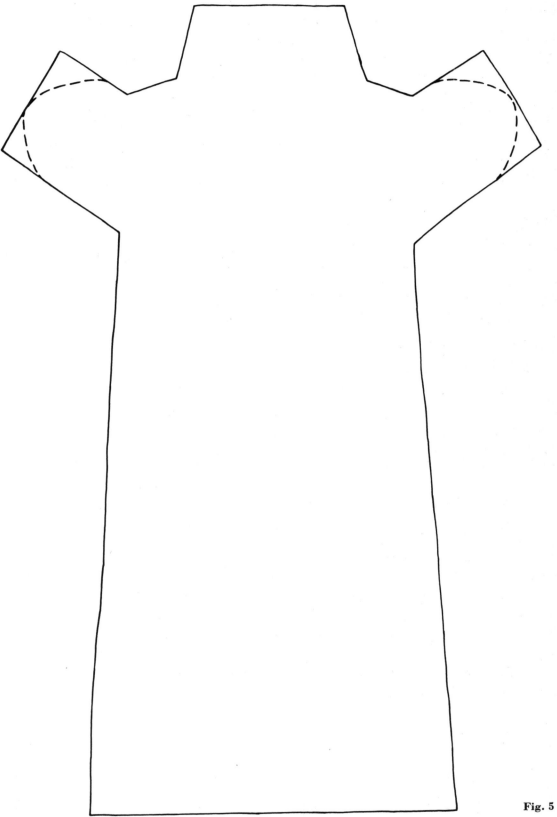

Fig. 5

The 'glove' or under-garment

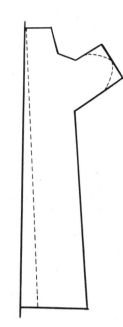

Basically, a hand puppet is no more than a head and a 'glove' or sack. Since the latter forms the 'body', it is obvious that the design of this major portion of the puppet requires some thought. Any cloth bag, with holes made in it for the fingers, would probably be both restrictive and uncomfortable to the puppeteer.

The glove should be roomy, but it should not hang in folds. It should fit the wearer comfortably, yet enable the maximum of control.

The basic design given at Fig. 5 is recommended for general use, but it should be adjusted up or down according to the wearer.

Cut out a paper pattern. For a larger hand size expand the back with a gusset, the point of which should finish just below the neckline. Another method is to fold both the paper pattern and the cloth material. Lay the back folded edge of the pattern along the fold of the material. Place a finger firmly on the neck of the pattern and, using this as a pivot point, swing the pattern an inch or so away from the folded edge of the material. When you have increased the size sufficiently, continue to hold the pattern firmly in this position, while marking it out on the material. Now cut out the pattern before unfolding the material. See Fig. 6. To reduce the hand size, make a dart in the front section, with the point also coming just below the neckline. See Fig. 7. The size of the neck should remain constant.

Fig. 6

The open end of the arm, shown in Fig. 5, is for use with the wire and felt hands described in the next section. The dotted line shown in Fig. 5 is suggested for use with the mitt type hands, also described in the following section.

Fig. 7

Use a smooth, cool, but strong, material for the undergarment. Cotton broadcloth is excellent for this purpose and inexpensive.

When the two halves of the pattern are sewn together, do not turn inside out, as the raised seams would be uncomfortable to the wearer. When the puppet is finally costumed, and the costume seams are turned to the inside, both sets of seams will then be isolated between the two layers of material, as in any lined garment.

Turn in the neck-edge about half an inch and run a double gathering thread through the two thicknesses. This will be finished off later, when the head is attached to the body.

Do not at this point hem the bottom of the garment.

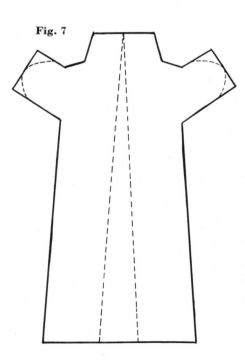

The hands

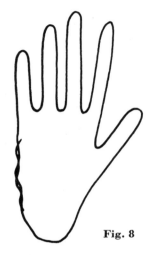

Fig. 8

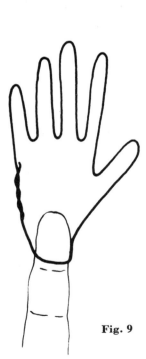

Fig. 9

Wire and felt hands

This type of hand enables the arms of the puppet to be considerably longer without losing control of the hands.

For this hand leave the glove arms open at the end, as shown at Fig. 5. Fig. 8 shows the shape to which a piece of stove-pipe wire is worked to form the basis for the hand.

Spread the fingers slightly and lay the wire frame on a piece of white felt and draw the shape on the felt with a pencil. Repeat this again with the same frame. Leave an adequate length of felt at the wrist. Cut out both hand shapes and set them aside with the frame. Do not attempt to cut the two shapes from one tracing on a piece of doubled felt.

Repeat the process, using the frame for the second hand. Keep each set of felt hands and their frame together, as a mix-up will result in a misfit.

Now bend the rounded end of the wire frames to fit around the appropriate finger or thumb of the hand on which the puppet is to be worn, as shown at Fig. 9.

Oversew the edges of the felt, starting and stopping temporarily at the base of the little finger or the thumb.

Put the wire frame into position in the fingers.

Stuff the fingers and palm with kapok and then complete the sewing down both sides of the hand.

Sew the hands in a comfortable position in the open end of the arms.

It is advisable to paint the hands before costuming the puppet.

The wire bent around the fingers will be found to give a good purchase and strength for the handling of properties.

It may also be found to be more comfortable if suitable-sized bankers' rubber finger-stalls are glued into the ends of the hands after they have been sewn in position on the arms. This is according to individual preference.

The length of the arms can be extended another two inches or so by increasing the length of the wire frame. This will aid effect, but means a loss of control and strength for the handling of properties.

Mitt hands

This is a very simple type of hand, but although effective enough, the arms of the puppet are necessarily restricted in length to enable sufficient control of the hands for the picking up of properties, etc.

Fig. 10 shows a suitable design for a mitt hand for use with the glove design at Fig. 5.

Cut the mitts out of felt, preferably white because it can be painted later.

Sew the two sections of each mitt together and turn inside out.

Round off the ends of the arms of the glove, as shown by the dotted lines at Fig. 5.

The mitts may be padded out with kapok before being sewn in position over the ends of the arms.

The shape of the fingers may also be sewn into the mitts if desired.

Paint the hands before costuming the puppet.

Fig. 10

Attaching the head

The head is usually attached to the undergarment before the costume is put on. This enables a final fitting to be made for the comfort of the hand before the costume is completely attached to the puppet. The undergarment and the hands are then pushed down through the hole in the neck of the costume and the costume pulled up into position, while the neck is still unfinished.

To attach the head, place the neck in the opening at the top of the undergarment and glue in position. Make sure the head is square on the body and not inclined to look to one side. Finally, pull the gathering threads as tightly as possible above the rim on the bottom of the neck and wind the excess thread tightly around so that it also becomes glued to the neck. The amount of glue that permeates the material will make the addition of more glue unnecessary.

Costume

The costume should follow the same basic pattern as the under-garment. Any type of costume may be used, based on the under-garment pattern for fit and length.

When the costume has been pulled on to the puppet by the method described previously, the neck-line should be gathered to fit closely over the edge of the under-garment, after which any type of collar may be fitted around the neck.

The sleeves may be gathered or left loose, according to costume requirements. If left loose, they should be finished with a hem.

The final stage of costuming is the turning-in and sewing together of the lower edges of both the costume and the under-garment. This provides a neat finish and ensures that the hand cannot be placed between the under-garment and the costume.

It is a good idea to sew a curtain ring on the bottom of each puppet costume at the back. This enables the puppet to be suspended on a hook when not in use during a show and the hand can quickly dive inside the costume as it hangs when the puppet is to be used. This is especially useful if there is already a puppet on the other hand.

Articulating the mouth

A hand puppet with a moving mouth is seldom called for in live performance, except for dragons and such creatures.

For those occasions when a mouth needs to be articulated the following methods will be found effective.

Method using the whole hand

This is the usual system used for dragons, alligators and other creatures having an unusually large mouth. Figure 11 shows the position of the hand inside the head of the puppet.

An old sock, cut open along the length of the foot and with two pieces of cardboard covered with felt stitched in the opening, makes a good basis for the operation of this type of mouth. Two pieces of thin plywood, hinged together, can be used in place of the cardboard.

Fig. 11

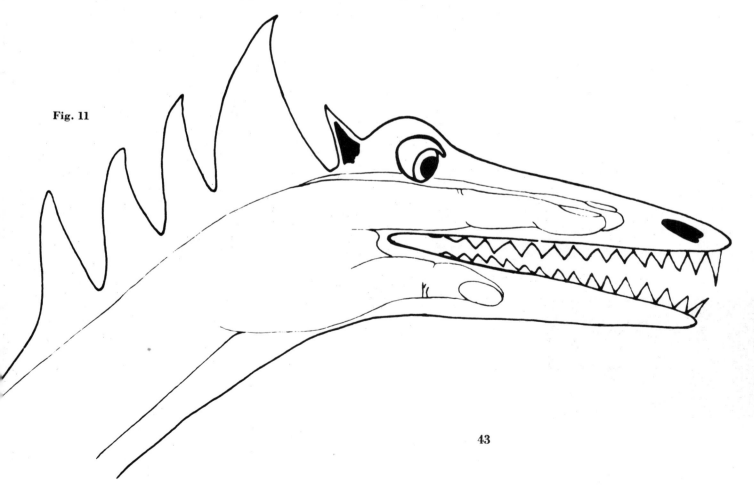

43

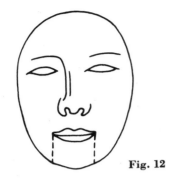

Fig. 12

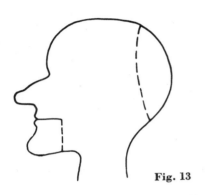

Fig. 13

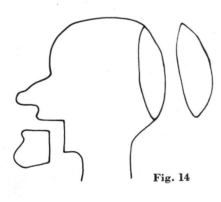

Fig. 14

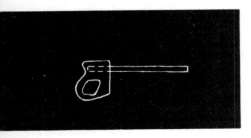

Fig. 15

Method of constructing a mouth operated by a string

It is easier to construct a moving mouth in a head that is made of plastic wood. Make the neck fatter than usual when modelling so that there is plenty of room for the new parts. Complete the joining of the head before putting in the mouth, but leave the neck open. The 'stopper' is put in later.

Draw guiding lines for cutting out the mouth as shown in Fig. 12. Fig. 13 shows the side view of the mouth and also the area to be cut out of the back of the head to afford access for working inside the head.

A sharp, thin-bladed knife is the best tool for cutting out the jaw. A fine back saw or a coping saw may be used to remove the back of the head. This section has eventually to be replaced, so keep it in a safe place and do not sweep it up with the shavings. Fig. 14 shows the jaw and back of the head removed.

Fig. 15 shows a flat piece of soft wood (approx. ¼ inch thick) set in the curve on the inside of the jaw. Hollow out as much of the inside of the jaw as is safe and insert a piece of lead when fixing the tongue. This will increase response. Use glue and plastic wood to fix the tongue in position. Set the jaw back in the head while the tongue dries, supporting the tongue from the back if necessary to keep it as horizontal as possible. Do not handle until thoroughly dry.

When dry note the line of the tongue through the head by inspection. Mark the position of the axle near the front of the face with a pencil, as shown in Fig. 16. Using a sharp awl, ease it through the wall of the head and mark the centre of the tongue opposite the hole.

Sharpen a length of 14-gauge wire, or preferably a bicycle spoke, using a metal file. The wire should be two or three inches longer than the width of the face.

Remove the jaw from the head and, placing the tongue in a vise, carefully drill a hole, at the point already marked, large enough to accommodate the wire comfortably. Take care not to drill at an angle.

Replace the jaw in the head and, holding it firmly in position, push the wire through the side of the head and the tongue; then, with the aid of a pair of pliers, work the point of the wire carefully through the other side of the face.

Only after this operation is completed, again remove the jaw and cut away a little of the neck, as shown in Fig. 17, below the original cut made for the removal of the jaw section.

The final amount of movement in the jaw is regulated by the amount cut away at this point. When sufficient movement has been gained, remove the wire and take out the jaw once more.

The teeth can now be modelled with plastic wood. It is advisable to model the top set first.

44

Place a small roll of plastic wood inside and protruding just below the top lip. Flatten this out and hold in position with the thumb, through the hole in the back of the head, while making the indentations to mark the teeth with a knife or modelling tool.

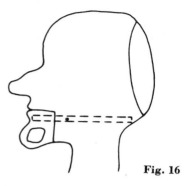

Fit the jaw in again in order to be sure the teeth do not get flattened by the front of the tongue. (It will be noticed in Fig. 16 that the tongue is set below the level of the lower lip in order to avoid this happening.)

Allow this set to dry for a short while and then model the lower set on the tongue so that they close just behind the top set.

Fig. 16

Allow the teeth to dry thoroughly before handling the jaw piece again.

The need for modelling a larger neck now becomes apparent.

To ensure a clean, sure mouth movement it is necessary to provide a separate passage for the string to a point below the bottom of the neck, in addition to the usual 'stopper' for the finger. This passage is built into the front of the neck, but at a point to the rear of the tongue pivot.

It is advisable to use a fairly thick string for the control in order that it may withstand some wear and not require frequent replacement. The passage for the string can be made from a short piece of rubber tubing, a piece of stiff spring, or anything else that suits the purpose. The tongue will need to be shortened to a point about an inch from the pivot, but it is wise to experiment before cutting it off too short.

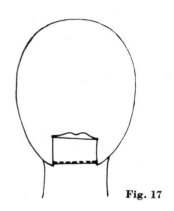

The tube for the string is set in the neck with glue and plastic wood and then the 'stopper' is placed in position behind it, using the same means. The hole in the back of the head facilitates the carrying out of these operations.

Fig. 17

Fig. 18 shows a side view of the tube, stopper and string in position. The position of the screw-eye in the under part of the tongue should be noted in relationship to the pivot and the tube. It may be necessary to adjust the position of the screw-eye before final attachment of the string is made. When all is complete, the string should be knotted very tightly to prevent it pulling loose from the screw-eye. A touch of strong glue on the knot is a worth-while precaution.

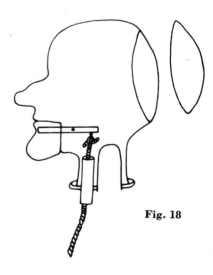

Leave the string long until the required length is known after the puppet is completed.

Make sure that the weight of the mouth is sufficient to drop it open immediately the tension on the string is relaxed. If there is any sluggishness in this movement it is possible to correct it by fastening a small, flat piece of lead near the front of the tongue, which will give it a sharper movement. (This should not be done until the lower set of teeth have been modelled on the tongue.)

Fig. 18

When the mouth mechanism is working correctly, shorten the pivot wire until it is flush with the sides of the head. Reinforce with plastic wood the insides of the face at the points where the wire enters; work through the hole in the back.

Finally cover the outside ends of the wire with plastic wood and glue the back of the head in position. Leave the head to dry thoroughly before further handling.

The head is mounted on the body in the usual way with the mouth control string carried through the costume to a convenient point below.

This type of mouth control is specially recommended when great accuracy of movement is required, but it means that the puppeteer needs both hands to operate the puppet.

Mouth movement by direct control

This movement is easier to construct, but is not quite so simple to operate accurately. It does, however, require only one hand.

It is also unnecessary to make the neck any larger than usual since there is not an extra passage for the string. The regular stopper is also discarded for this system of mouth movement, so leave the neck quite open for the time being.

Proceed with the cutting of the mouth and the positioning of the tongue, as for the string-controlled mouth, up to and including the step at Fig. 17. The teeth are then modelled in as previously described.

Glue layers of felt into the neck until it is possible to insert the index finger only as far as the second joint. This is similar to the rubber ball head principle described earlier.

Place the finger in the neck and mark the tongue at a point just in front of the tip of the finger, but *behind* the pivot.

Remove the jaw and shorten the tongue to the mark.

Place a B.4 screw-eye in the end of the tongue, at a downward angle, so that the end of the finger can operate the mouth by pressure on the screw-eye. Fig. 19 shows the operation of this mouth movement.

When the movement is satisfactory, shorten the pivot wire and finish the head in exactly the same way as for the string controlled mouth.

Both these methods can be used for animal heads as well as for human type heads.

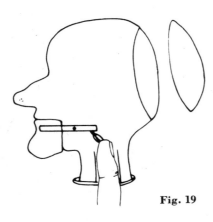

Fig. 19

Hand puppets with legs and feet

Fig. 20 shows the appearance of a hand puppet when it is desired to give it legs and feet.

The sleeve protruding from the back of the puppet should be quite long and preferably of a black material.

The hand forms the body and arms as previously, but the legs and feet can be made of cloth filled with kapok. They are not directly controlled.

Cut the patterns very 'full' and turn the legs inside out before filling.

Fig. 21 shows how the joints for the knees can be made by sewing seams at the appropriate places. Ankle joints can be treated in the same way if they are thought to be necessary. Wooden legs and feet can also be used if desired. The joints can be of cloth or leather glued into slots made in the wood. The leather or cloth at the top of the legs are sewn to the costume. In 'The Marionette' the construction of legs is described in some detail.

It will probably be found an advantage to weight the feet slightly so that they respond easily to being thrown over the playboard when the puppet is to sit on it.

Fig. 20

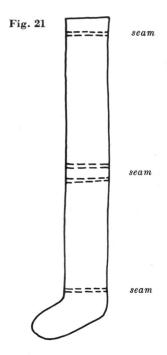

Fig. 21

seam

seam

seam

Manipulation

The hand puppet has basically few movements.

The main head movement is a nodding motion.

The arms will move forwards easily and to some extent up and down.

The body, of course, can twist in any direction and bend forwards and backwards with ease.

A review of these limitations may lead one to think that little can be effected by way of movement with these puppets, but nothing could be further from the truth. With practice and a skilful blending and modulation of the main movements, coupled with the puppet's natural ability to handle properties, it becomes the most versatile creature imaginable. Its movement, like its appearance, is full of fantasy, and this gives it a tremendous charm.

Never insult it by jigging it up and down, or nodding its head vigorously when it is speaking. This makes it appear quite ridiculous — and must inevitably hurt its dignity.

Treat it with consideration and give it movements that clearly indicate what it is portraying or doing. Separate the movements so that the audience can follow the actions as clearly as the words. Nothing is intelligible that is all run in together as though on a spring.

Practise miming a simple story and have the puppet put on a bold front, be frightened or bashful, as necessary. Act, act, act! Don't bounce, jiggle and wave!

It can only be interesting to the manipulator if the puppet is acting. Loss of interest by the manipulator is immediately evident in the puppet.

Practise the basic movements and then variations of them. Let the puppet make light work of a job and then find another job which is more difficult. Make it convey this extreme change by simulating puffing and panting and the worry of it.

Don't lose any of the possible effect by not holding the puppet up high enough. Always keep a good part of its body in view.

Never crowd a play with words. Give the puppet plenty of scope for acting and action. These two things are not synonymous.

Lastly, do not blame the puppet. It is only an instrument in your hands. If things are not going well, look to your own failings. The puppet is only as good an actor as you are.

Staging

The two principal types of hand puppet presentation require a somewhat different stage set-up, although it is possible to design a stage that is adaptable to both methods.

Briefly, one type of presentation is given with the manipulator behind the puppets and looking through a 'scrim' or semi-transparent material. The other is the system whereby the puppets are held up and worked at a level above the operator's head. Both have advantages. The stage for the scrim method can be smaller and therefore a little more portable, but the overhead presentation allows the puppets far greater mobility and the obvious advantages of scenic and lighting effects in depth.

The basic difference in the construction of these stages is mainly one of height, but the overhead operation may also need a little more depth.

For the scrim stage the playboard is constructed at chest height and for the other, slightly above the head.

Obviously, if the puppets are using properties that require exacting manipulation, then this will be made easier if the manipulator is able to see them through the scrim, when they are then immediately in the line of vision. For many shows, however, particularly if there is an element of fantasy, the overhead operation will be the most effective.

Basically, the hand puppet stage is a simple affair. It is merely a three-sided screen, which hides the manipulator, with an opening in the upper half of the centre section through which the puppets are seen. Add to this a playboard, the board above which the puppets work and on which properties rest, a back-cloth, some front curtains to draw between the acts and a ledge below the playboard to hold the properties and store the puppets ready for use. The lighting can be very simple, particularly for the stage using a scrim back-cloth.

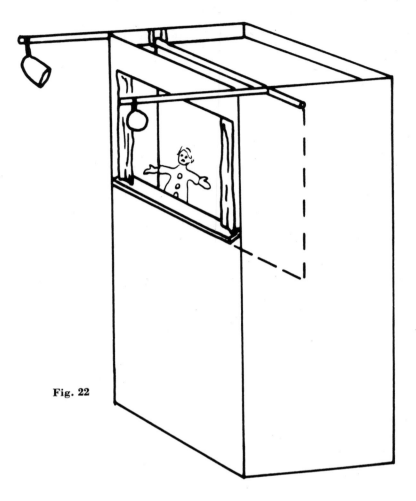

Fig. 22

Stage with scrim back-cloth

Fig. 22 shows the front view of a stage with a scrim background. It will be noticed that this background is fairly close to the front of the stage in order that the operator may stand behind it and still reach the playboard easily. It could, however, be made adjustable to varying distances from the playboard if this were felt necessary. To do this easily there should be a series of slots into which the rod holding the back-cloth can be slipped. Usually two positions are sufficient for this stage.

It is a good idea to plan a stage with a proscenium opening not less than four feet wide and two feet high. Any enlargement of this opening would be in width rather than height. Many otherwise good shows are spoiled through being too cramped. Three feet is sufficient depth for the sides of this stage and the total height need not exceed 6½ feet. This will also allow the proscenium opening to be set high enough in the stage front for good viewing.

The stage framework can be made of any suitable material, but they are usually of wood, aluminum piping or aluminum angle strips. Wood stages are usually made up of six wooden frames pin-hinged together to either fold in pairs or take completely apart. Sometimes the masking material is stretched over and tacked permanently to each of the frames, or it may be hung from screw-eyes placed at the top, using regular drapery hooks, and the material draped in folds. This method gives the stage a better appearance.

Of the piping stages, aluminum is easily the best because of its light weight. Pipe is preferable to tubing since it has a heavier wall for threading and it is possible to buy standard threaded fittings such as elbow, tee and straight joining pieces, made from aluminum, iron or copper. Straight joining may also be achieved by the sleeve method, in which a smaller gauge of pipe or solid rod is 'sweated' inside the end of the tube, leaving about three or four inches protruding. This is then pushed into the open end of the extension tube, as shown at Fig. 23.

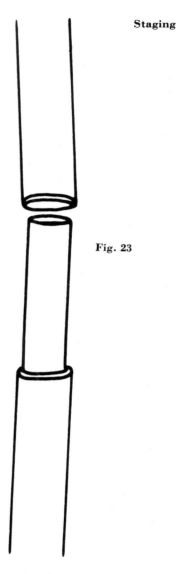

Fig. 23

Slotted aluminum angle strip can be purchased in lengths of about ten feet. This material can be cut to the desired size with a hack saw and the framework can then be bolted together very easily. Angle strip is very versatile in that it can be extended by merely bolting on the desired extra lengths. The masking drapes are easily hooked on to the many holes and slots along the length of the strips.

The playboard should be about six inches wide and placed in the proscenium so that at least half of it is set back inside the stage. This enables properties to be clipped to the board when necessary while the front curtains are closed.

Scenery may be painted on the scrim back-cloth as required, without interfering with the operator's view. A neutral-coloured scrim should be used, with tempera or fabric paints. Naturally, these scrims must be changed for different backgrounds, so it is worth while having an easy slotting device for quick changes. If the operator is visible through a scrim, a single piece of black nylon chiffon hung behind the scrim will correct this.

The properties board is clearly shown in Fig. 24. The row of cup-hooks are for puppet storage and quick use.

Any of the standard drapery tracks are recommended for the front draw-curtains.

Lighting

Lighting for this stage is better placed outside the proscenium. If installed inside, the limited depth of the stage causes the light to be too much over the heads of the puppets, which results in the lower part of the faces being in shadow. Fig. 22 shows the suggested positioning of the lights. It is more effective to have them hinged to the top of the stage so that they can be swung out and adjusted both for best effect and to avoid blinding the operator behind the scrim. Do not neglect, where possible, opportunities to use all the devices of theatrical lighting such as coloured gelatines and dimmers.

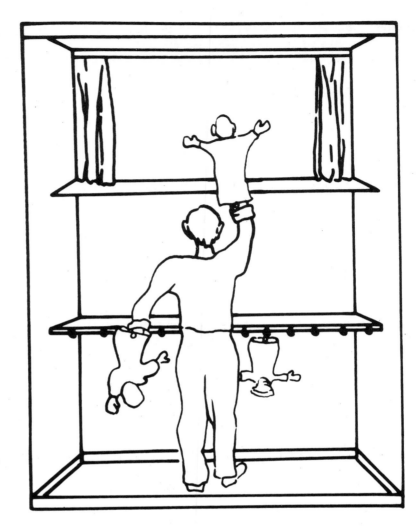

Fig. 24

Stage for overhead operation

Fig. 24 shows the rear view and general arrangement of a stage built for overhead operation. Basically it is the same as for the stage just described, but generally speaking it should be at least five feet wide if full advantage is to be had from its use.

Proportionate to the depth of the stage a great deal of effect can be gained by introducing a series of wings at intervals from the front to the back.

Additional lighting can also be introduced inside the stage.

Heavier drapes and sets can be used in this stage since the manipulators do not have to see through them.

The height of the playboard will depend on the height of the tallest person expected to work with it.

Properties that stand on the playboard and could easily be upset should either be mounted on a wide base of thin plywood or be fitted with a wire that will clip to the back edge of the playboard. See Fig. 25. It is better to use coat-hanger wire than galvanized wire, because it is more resilient. Sometimes it is more convenient to drill small holes in the playboard and peg the properties in place.

If a playboard is made to be easily removable it is possible to have a separate playboard for certain plays or scenes upon which the properties are firmly mounted. This would only be necessary if the properties involved were numerous and required exact positioning.

As a general rule do not spare the use of properties with hand puppets because they handle them well and add a great deal to the interest.

Fig. 25

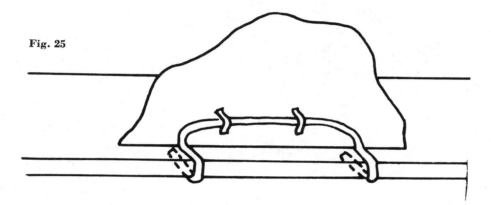

A variety of puppets in the same show

Do not hesitate to mix the types of puppets you use, not only in the same show, but at the same time, if it achieves the effect you require.

A shadow screen can easily be installed at the back of a hand puppet stage designed for overhead working. Both black and white and colour effects can be obtained in the background while hand and/or rod puppets work in front. (See the section on shadow puppets for details of shadow construction and manipulation.)

A large number of special effects can be obtained in this way. The lighting of the puppets working in front need not interfere with the brightness of the shadow screen, nor need they appear as silhouettes against the screen, although this could sometimes be very effective.

A shadow screen could also be combined with the scrim type of stage if the manipulator sat down low enough to be able to work above the head, as in the overhead stage. In this event the screen could be set towards the back of the stage in order to give the puppet manipulator more room.

53

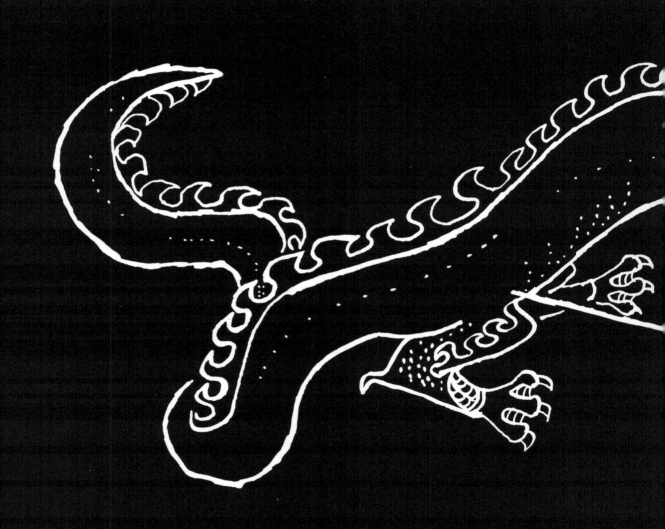

Hand and rod puppets

Rod puppets

Sock puppets

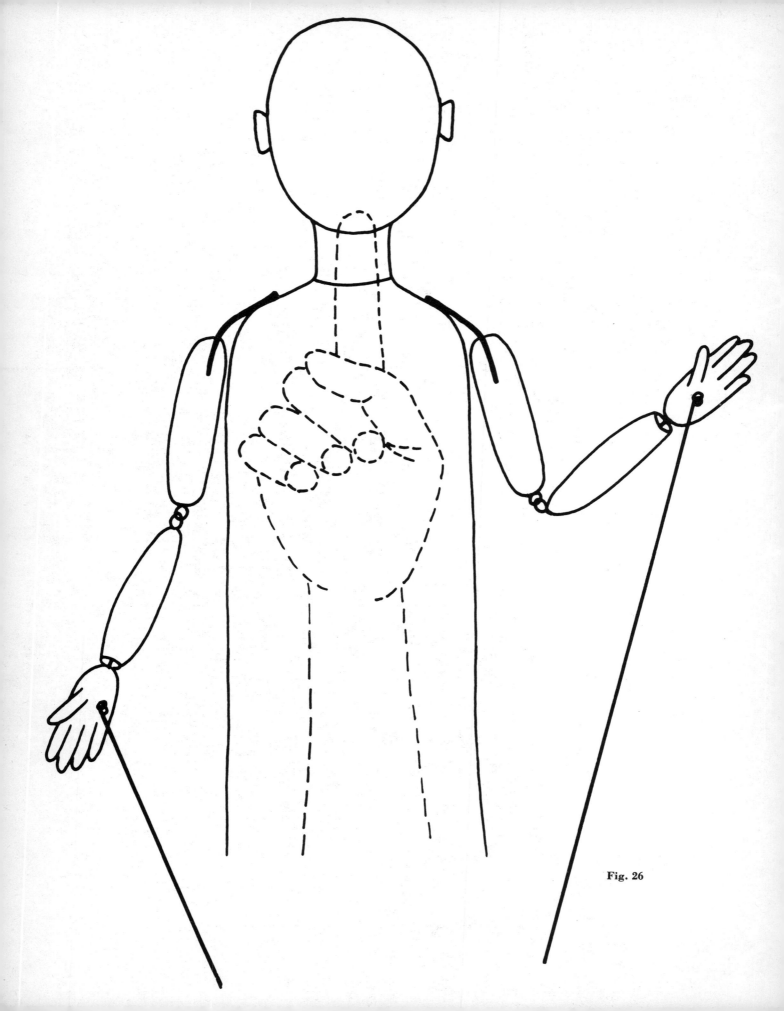

Fig. 26

Hand and rod puppets

The chief advantage of this type of puppet is in the amount of expression that may be obtained from the movements of the arms, which can be of any length and are controlled by means of wires or rods attached to the puppet's hands.

At the same time, this arrangement makes the handling of properties very difficult and, unlike a regular hand puppet, properties would usually have to be attached to the hands off-stage.

The wires also restrict some of the movements that are obtainable from a hand puppet.

Best use can be made of hand and rod puppets in dramatic presentations, certain types of dance movements, singing and restricted clowning.

The head of the puppet may be manipulated by the forefinger, in the same way as a hand puppet, or by means of a long dowel glued inside the neck, which is gripped by the hand.

It is necessary for the puppeteer to use both hands for the successful operation of the hand and rod puppet. One hand controls the head, whichever of the above methods is used, while the two arm-control wires are manipulated by the other hand.

Fig. 26 shows a hand and rod puppet with the head manipulated by the forefinger. In use the operator's hand will give the body some shape. The puppet's arms are jointed at the shoulders, elbows and wrists. If necessary, the shoulders could be given some padding.

Fig. 27 shows the dowel head control with the dowel passing through a hole in the wooden shoulder piece. This allows for considerable head movement. A large washer attached to the dowel just below the shoulder piece will regulate the amount of upward stretch in the neck. A thin dowel through the neck dowel will also achieve this purpose.

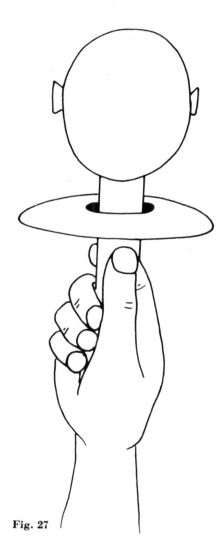

Fig. 27

Hand and rod puppets

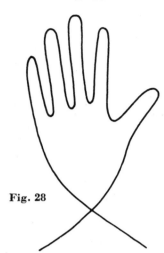

Fig. 28

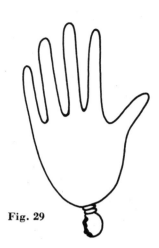

Fig. 29

Fig. 30

Fig. 31

Fig. 32

Hands

Wooden or felt hands may be used. The wire shape for the felt hand is shown at Figs. 28 and 29.

Shape the hands from stove pipe wire, but do not make them too large.

Start the shaping at the little finger, but leave at least 6″ spare for finishing.

Make sure the loop of wire formed at the wrist is no more than ¼″ in diameter.

For preference make the hands from white felt, so that they can be painted later.

Spread the wire fingers slightly, then lay the frame on a piece of felt and trace the shape twice.

Cut out the hands and oversew the edges, starting at the little finger. When the top of the thumb is reached, push the wire into the glove and stuff the fingers and palm with kapok before completing the sewing.

Fig. 30 shows a hand shape outlined on a block of wood.

Cut away the shaded parts outside the heavy lines.

Chisel away the shaded portion of the thumb to approximately the level in Fig. 31, which shows a side view of the hand.

Always work at the inside shape of the palm before finishing the shape of the back of the hand. This will lessen the chances of a finger breaking off during the operation.

Fig. 32 shows an under-glove similar to that for a hand puppet, but minus the arms. The methods of enlarging or reducing this glove are the same as those described on page 39.

Arms

The puppet's arms can be made of wood, cloth sleeves filled with kapok, string, soft wire spring, or any other suitable material.

Thin leather, or strong cloth, strips should be inserted and glued at the tops of the wooden arms. These tabs can then be sewn to the shoulder positions of the under-glove.

Linked B2 screw-eyes can be used for the elbow joints.

Holes should be drilled into the ends of the lower arms large enough to take the wire loops or screw-eyes on the hands.

B2 screw-eyes should be put in at the wrists of wooden hands.

Both wooden and felt hands are attached to the lower arms by inserting the screw-eyes, or wire loops, as the case may be, into the holes at the wrists and pinning them in position from the sides of the arms. Fig. 33 shows the shoulder, elbow and wrist joints.

If cloth arms are used enough extra length of material should be allowed for all the joints, including the tabs at the shoulders.

Fig. 33 shows how seams are sewn to form the joints. The seams for the tabs at the shoulders should be sewn at right angles to the seams at the elbows.

If wooden hands are used, slots should be made at the wrists. The flat, seamed ends of the cloth arms are inserted in the slots and glued in position.

The wire loops on felt hands can be inserted in the ends of cloth arms and sewn in position.

All these joints have some play at the wrists, but care should be taken that there is not so much play that they are hard to control.

Small loops should be made at one end of each of the control wires. These should be loosely sewn to the cloth hands. They are usually attached to the palms, but may be jointed at any point that suits the action.

To attach the controls to wooden hands, the simplest method is to put A1 screw-eyes in the hands and link the wires to them.

The control wires must not be fixed rigidly to the hands, but must be free to move easily, in the manner of a universal joint.

Some very elegant costuming is possible with hand and rod puppets.

Manipulation, particularly of the arms, can be controlled to a fine degree.

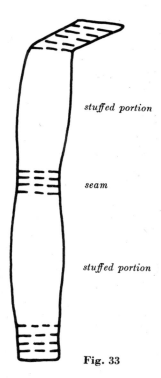

stuffed portion

seam

stuffed portion

Fig. 33

Rod puppets

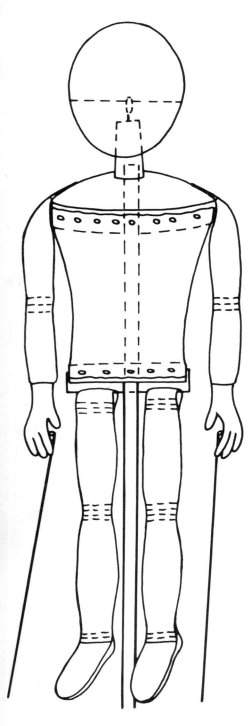

Fig. 34

Depending on their construction rod puppets can be reasonably versatile, or somewhat restricted in their movements. The construction ranges from flat cut-out figures, mounted on sticks, to fully fashioned puppets with many joints.

Some types of rod puppets give the impression of being almost mechanical in their operation. Certain presentations, such as Bible stories and serious narrative plays, may be done very effectively with these puppets, particularly when the majority of the movements are made by the head and arms, both of which can be controlled to an exacting degree. When using these puppets a great deal of attention should be given to stage lighting and presentation generally. This helps to offset any limitations and over-stylization of movement.

Although construction variations are legion, the basic principle used in these puppets is a wooden column, which is attached to the head or shoulder piece — which arrangement gives the head more freedom — and control wires that operate the various parts of the body. These wires are either external to the body or are designed in conjunction with the main column and are concealed beneath the costume.

Weight is always a problem with rod puppets if they are of any size; there is no limit as to size, but often a body can be dispensed with and the costume draped from the shoulder piece.

In operation the column is held in one hand, or plugged or slotted in a special position on a shelf below the playboard. The wire control levers, which are arranged at the base of the column, are manipulated with the other hand, or with both hands when they are free. Umbrella spokes are often used for the control wires.

If the control wires are external to the body, one is usually placed at the back of the head and others are attached to the hands.

Strings are occasionally used as well as wires to operate rod puppets. The strings have to be conveyed below, so care must be taken that they do not pass over any roughly made parts or they will need constant repair.

Rod puppets sometimes have legs, which can either swing free or be controlled by wires or strings. Fig. 34 shows a puppet of this type.

The body is made of cloth, stuffed with kapok, which is glued and tacked to a wooden shoulder piece. The lower part of the body is attached in the same manner to an oval-shaped piece of wood, which should also be thick enough to take the wires from which the legs are suspended.

Fig. 35 is a side view of the way the head is mounted on the neck by means of a screw-eye and a piece of wire, preferably a bicycle spoke, and it also shows how the head control wire is attached.

The legs and arms are of stuffed cloth. See Fig. 33 for method.

The hands may be of wood or felt. See Figs. 28, 29, 30 and 31.

The feet can be cut out of cloth as an extension of the legs, or they can be made of wood.

A more simple type of rod puppet, very fluid in movement, can be made using wire springs as the basis of its construction. Toy 'slinkeys' are very useful in this regard.

The control wires are loosely attached directly to the springs at points designed to give the best control and greatest possible amount of movement. The caterpillar, shown in the Photofolio section, is an example of this type of puppet.

Rod puppets are operated from below and so require a stage very similar to a hand puppet stage. A greater amount of space in the wings would be an advantage and also a special shelf would be necessary if the puppets are to be supported.

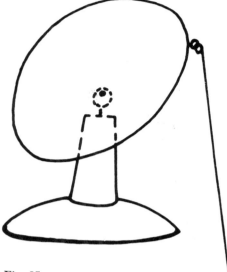

Fig. 35

61

Sock puppets

These are a novelty type of puppet, but a great deal of fun can be had with them. They lend themselves to animal or bird characters more readily than to human. Because they are made from soft materials and are operated with the hand inside the head, in the same way as the dragon at Fig. 11, it is very easy to give these puppets many changes of expression by movements of the hand.

Usually the puppet consists only of a head. The amount of animation gained from manipulating the face causes the absence of legs or arms to pass unnoticed. They are also very effective used as regular hand puppets in animal plays and ideal for use on playgrounds and in similar situations.

These puppets can be made very quickly and the only material requirements are a sock, needle and thread, scissors, and various trim materials, such as felt, buttons, drapery fringe, sequins and other odds and ends. Plain socks are probably best for these puppets, but some sock patterns will suggest ideas for characters.

The mouths or beaks are formed by using either the heel or the foot of the sock. The ears are also formed from the foot or the heel, depending on which is being used for the mouth. Ears can also be made from pieces of felt, if it fits the character, or from other suitable materials, which are sewn in position later. A floppy-eared dog, for instance, looks well with felt ears.

In Fig. 36 the dotted lines indicate the scissor cuts for the making of a dragon. When the cutting is completed, the sock should be turned inside out and the gap at the heel sewn across (not together) to form the ears.

Cut some stiff cardboard into a shape to fit easily into the opening at the foot. The cardboard should be folded in the middle to form the roof and bottom of the mouth, as shown at Fig. 37.

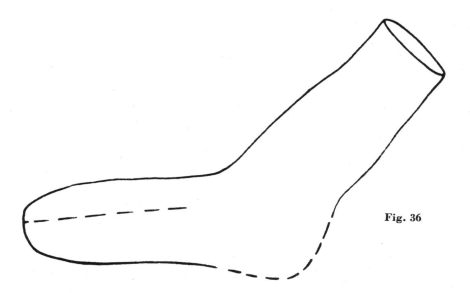

Fig. 36

Cover the cardboard with red felt, plush, or other material.

Turn the sock back to the right side out and sew the cardboard section into the mouth opening.

Use white felt, ric-rak, or large white sequins for the teeth.

Buttons make good eyes and any other trimming can be added as necessary to complete the character.

To shape the beak for a bird, or to gain any particular head shape, the sock may be cut as required. A head may be rounded by sewing into it a cloth bag filled with kapok.

Some examples of sock puppets will be found in the Photofolio section.

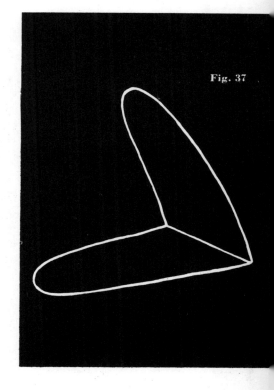

Fig. 37

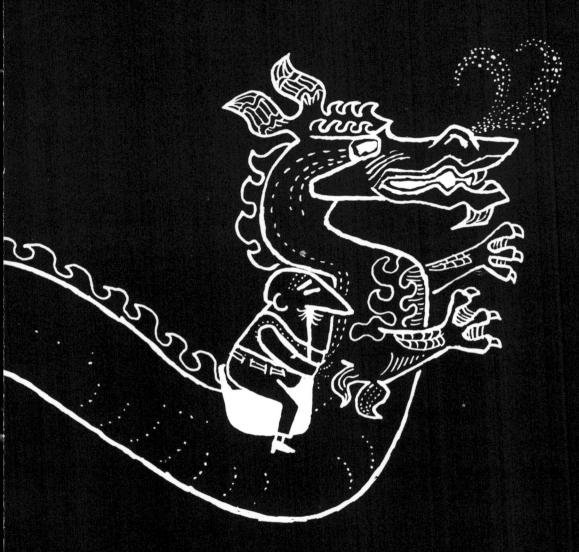

n. Finger puppets

Finger puppets

To many people finger puppets may appear to be novelties rather than practical puppets with many uses. But experiment will show that these little figures can be used for a great many purposes and in all manner of situations. The making of them will tax the ingenuity.

The size of finger puppets will, of course, vary with the size of the operator's hands, since the index and second fingers are the puppet's legs. By lengthening the legs, and by other devices, the puppets can be constructed to an average height of 8 or 9 inches. With good lighting these small puppets can be seen comfortably by many people. Even larger figures can be made by attaching the body of the puppet to the hand, just below the wrist, and faking the length of the legs.

Since material requirements are few and inexpensive, these little figures are ideal for use in the home, the school, the hospital and for intimate types of entertainment. Finger puppets are practical for both plays and variety presentations. It is possible for one operator to manipulate two puppets at the same time, using one on each hand.

The following pages contain basic information for the construction of finger puppets, but by a free use of the imagination some very fanciful figures can be created.

Construction

Materials

Finger puppets can be made from a variety of materials. The principle on which the action of the puppet is based is very simple and once this is appreciated there should be no difficulty in either making or using them.

The following basic materials will be needed to begin the construction of finger puppets. Add or substitute as you wish and do not limit yourself in the use of either materials or in design.

Length of 1″ x 2″ pine (approximately 4 bodies per foot)

Wooden, cork or table-tennis balls

Wooden meat skewers or lollipop sticks

½-inch dressmaker's elastic (7 or 8 inches per puppet)

Pipe cleaners

Carpet tacks

Needles and thread

Oil paint (20c. tubes) and brushes

Turpentine

Japan driers

Plastic wood

Glue

Petroleum jelly

Costume materials, including scraps of felt

Cardboard

Hand drill (with bit the same size as skewers)

Whittling knife

Scissors

No. 14 or 16 gauge wire

Adhesive tape

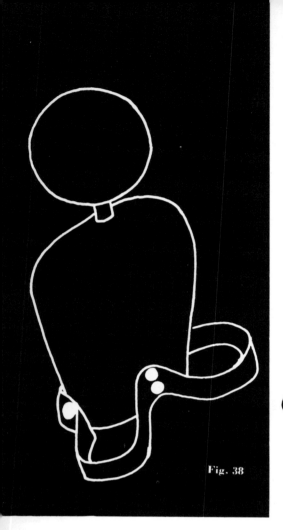

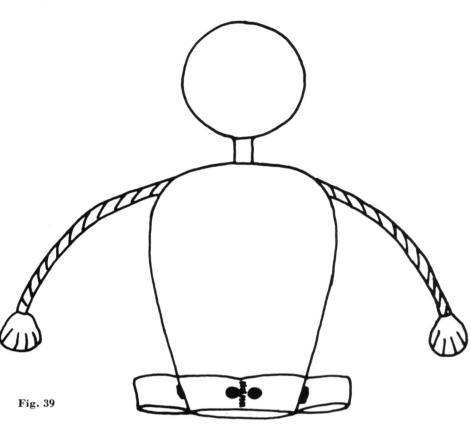

Fig. 38   Fig. 39

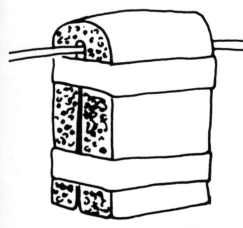

Fig. 40

Methods of constructing a body

Bodies can be made by whittling a piece of 1″ x 2″ pine into a rough shape and then attaching the elastic by means of glue and carpet tacks. See Figs. 38 and 39. Make the elastic a little tighter than is comfortable at first. It will stretch after some use.

Bodies can also be made by bending double a piece of foam rubber and binding it with adhesive tape (see Fig. 40), or by stuffing a small cloth bag. The elastic will have to be sewn and glued to these bodies since the carpet tacks would be of no use.

If a number of bodies of similar size are required it is a good idea to cast them in plastic wood or papier-mâché.

First model a body shape in plasticine. (It is as well to model and cast a round head at the same time.) Cut the body (and the head) in half with a piece of carpet warp, using it like a cheese wire. The body should be cut through the shoulders, not down the middle. Place these parts on a work-table, flat sides down, in a frame of suitable size. See Fig. 41. Mix some plaster-of-Paris according to the instructions given on page 12 and pour it into the mould. When the mould is dry, turn it over and remove the plasticine with a screw driver.

68

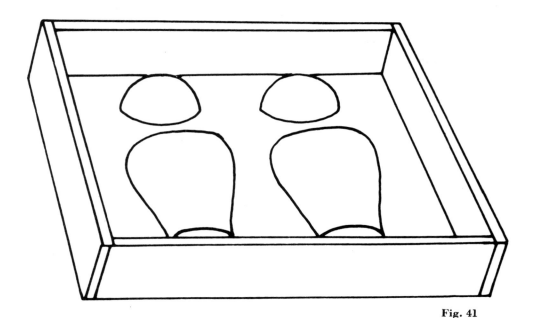

Fig. 41

Puppet bodies may be taken from the mould in either plastic wood or papier-mâché. Follow the instructions for both of these methods given on pages 12 and 24, or 28.

Papier-mâché can be dried in a warm place or with the aid of a heat lamp, but plastic wood must be left to dry at room temperature or in a heated place, but not near a flame or electric element.

When the body and head parts are thoroughly dry in the mould, they should be taken out and joined together as soon as possible. If they are left lying around after removal from the mould they may warp.

Trim the edges and sand them lightly, using a circular motion on a piece of sandpaper laid on a table.

Before joining the parts together, the neck piece and the arms should be prepared and placed in position. See Fig. 42. Plastic wood and glue are used to anchor both neck and arms to the body and head.

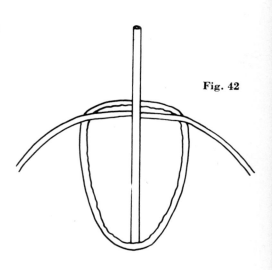

Fig. 42

To join the parts, glue all edges and then put a little plastic wood around one side only of the body and around one side only of the head. When this is done and the arms and neck are in position, put the body parts together and press tightly, with the neck protruding. Tie the body with string or use an elastic band to prevent separation. Place the two halves of the head around the neck, the length of the neck having been allowed for previously.

NOTE: When working with plastic wood rub some petroleum jelly into the hands to prevent the plastic wood from sticking.

Heads

Finger puppet heads can be made by the moulding process just described, or from cork, wooden balls, table-tennis balls, or any other suitable material. Ordinary bottle corks are useful for odd-shaped heads.

It is best to keep the amount of modelling on the head to a minimum. Often only the nose and ears need to be modelled. The rest can be defined with paint. Any modelling that is necessary can be done with plastic wood, papier-mâché, or the modelling compound described on page 32. Wool or theatrical crêpe makes good hair, or the hair may be painted on. Oil paints are the most satisfactory, but tempera colours can be used. Use turpentine and a little Japan driers for mixing the oil paint. This will ensure quicker drying.

Necks

The most useful material for necks are wooden meat skewers or lollipop sticks. The neck will be more rigid if the skewer is almost the length of the body and head. If foam rubber is used for the body, a plastic type of glue or rubber cement will be the best to use. The neck can be sewn and, if necessary, glued to a stuffed body. In a solid wood body, drill a hole for the neck and use ordinary wood glue. A length of pliable spring also makes a good neck for certain effects.

Arms

The arms are of two main types — fixed ones made of wire and covered with adhesive tape, pipe cleaners or other suitable material, and moveable arms made of parcel string. See Fig. 43.

The string arms are manipulated by means of black carpet warp attached to the hands and fastened to the ends of a short wooden bar. See Fig. 43. When the arms are made this way the operator requires both hands to use the puppet. In the case of wooden, plastic wood or mâché bodies, the string arms can be tied to small screw-eyes at the shoulders.

Wire arms should pass right through the body at the shoulders. With the moulded body this should be done when the halves of the body are joined together. See Fig. 42. When using foam rubber the wire can be put in before the body taping is done. The solid-wood body will have to be drilled and the wire glued in. The covering should be done after the wire is inserted in the body so that the shoulder will be neat. Covered wire arms can be adjusted to any desired position each time the puppet is used.

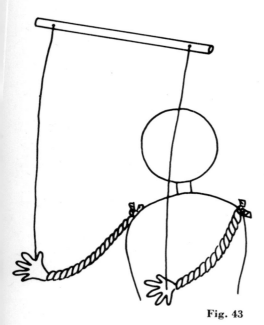

Fig. 43

Hands

The easiest way to make the hands is to model them in either plastic wood, papier-mâché, or the modelling compound, over the ends of the wire or string arms. In order that the hand material may 'grip' the arms, wire arms should be twisted into a small loop at the wrist and string arms tied in a knot. Make the arms long enough to do this when attaching them to the body. When dry the hands can be painted and the fingers defined with paint.

Adhesive tape may also be used for making hands, but plastic wood or papier-mâché will give more weight for control when string arms are used.

Feet

Most people's index and second fingers are of different lengths and these are the fingers used for the puppet's legs. If the puppet is to walk properly the legs need to be of equal length. Very satisfactory legs and feet can be made by rolling a piece of cardboard to a suitable size and length. Allowance should be made for one to fit a little more tightly on the shorter finger, so that it will not go on so far and thereby compensate for the difference in the length of the fingers. Some shape can also be given to the legs by having them taper a bit to the ankles.

Feet can be made by gluing or sewing flat pieces of felt across the bottom of the tubes. It is as well to use a double thickness of felt for this purpose. See Fig. 44. Felt can be used to build up the sides of boots or shoes if required. The legs may be painted or covered with any suitable material.

Ordinary rubber teapot spouts worn on the finger ends are also quite good for feet. By pushing the one on the second finger further up than the one on the index finger, the length of the legs can usually be equalized. Used at full length they will give the puppet added height. If the spouts are trimmed down almost to shoe size, leave the one intended for the index finger longer than the other one.

The spouts can be painted any colour. Rubber-based paint would be less liable to crack than oil paint.

If special shoe effects are required, these can be modelled over the ends of the cardboard tubes or the spouts with plastic wood or papier-mâché and later painted.

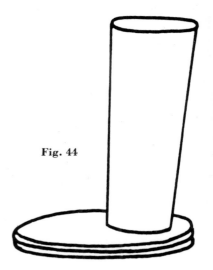

Fig. 44

Painting

Whatever material is used, paint the head a flesh colour after modelling the necessary features. Special characters may, of course, require a different base colour. Finger puppets' heads should be painted in fairly strong colours and the features clearly defined so that the head and face will 'carry' to the audience.

A satisfactory flesh colour can be made from White, Yellow Ochre and either Vermilion or Scarlet Lake. Add the red cautiously or it will predominate. Mix with turpentine. Drying time can be cut down by adding a very little Japan driers to the paint. If too much driers is used the paint will dry shiny. Make sure the paint is dry before putting on the hair. If desired, the hair may be painted on when the head is painted.

Costumes

As with the head, costume colours should be strong. Decoration should be well defined and not too detailed. On this scale of working the design and colours of the costumes must assist to 'project' the puppet.

Relatively heavy 'build-up' costumes such as layers of petticoats are quite permissible, and very effective, since the finger 'legs' can easily work against their weight and bulk. A long black glove, with the index and second fingers cut off, should be worn on the hand when operating. A black stocking, with two holes cut for the fingers, is a good substitute for a glove. Use of these will minimize the presence of the hand and will also accentuate the colours and size of the puppet.

Animals

It is possible to make interesting animal puppets by using a glove, with four of the fingers (or three fingers and the thumb) representing the animal's legs. In this way the animal, complete with head and tail, can be built up over the glove. An effective circus scene can be prepared by this method.

Manipulation

A finger puppet has relatively few movements, but despite this seeming handicap it is possible, with practice, to achieve a remarkable number of variations of these movements. Basically, walking is the puppet's chief movement and this is quite easy because it is not too difficult to control the fingers. Try all the variations of walking, forwards, backwards, sideways and also kicking. Running is an easy thing to do with these puppets. They can also stop suddenly and change direction and pace very quickly. They are quite versatile in the field of dancing and can do a very convincing splits. They can hop and jump with more control than any other puppet and can skate with ease. Some amusing acrobatic feats are also possible, and do not neglect the use of properties.

With practice, some very effective work can be done in both plays and variety with a puppet on each hand. The direct control makes the timing quite simple once co-ordination between the hands has been mastered.

Moving arms on a finger puppet adds a considerable variety to its stock of movements but, of course, it requires both hands to manipulate.

Explore all the possibilities and then practise.

Staging

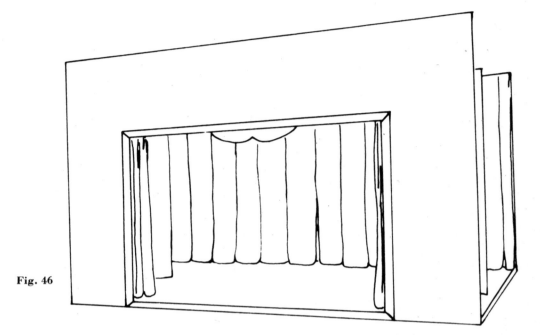

Fig. 46

Fig. 45

Finger puppets can be presented formally or informally. However, it is always preferable to cover the hands with black, as suggested earlier.

A table is usually at a good operating height and a small table-top theatre can be made by constructing a stage as shown in Fig. 45. The stage can be made larger or smaller, according to whether it is for one or several operators.

If desired, the front proscenium and draw curtains can be dispensed with, but the black background and the wings should be retained. A hanging drape suspended immediately above the front edge of the stage and low enough to conceal the operators, makes a good substitute for a proscenium. See Fig. 46.

If 1-inch board is used for the stage floor the stage is less likely to 'creep' while the show is on.

A simple and quick way to create and dismantle the stage is to use a system of dowel pegs to fit the parts together. See details in Figs. 47 and 48. The most satisfactory construction material is ¼-inch plywood, reinforced by wooden slats.

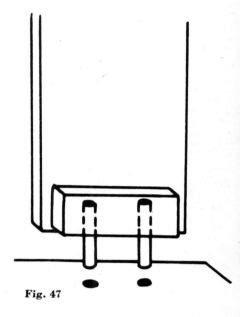

Fig. 47

Lighting

Lighting is as important a feature of the finger-puppet presentation as it is of any other stage show. By concentrating the light as much as possible on the acting area and avoiding 'spill', the puppets' actions will not only carry further, but the puppets themselves will tend to look larger.

Coloured lighting can be very effective and, where there is no proscenium and front curtain, a 'blackout' is a good means of changing stage properties.

Special effects

After the initial experiments a great many ideas will come to mind for novelty acts.

Interesting 'black light' effects can be attained by using a 250-watt purple lamp. This lamp is very reasonable to buy, and quite adequate for this type of show. It will fit a standard socket and will last about 50 hours. Any hardware store can supply it, although it will probably have to be specially ordered. Fluorescent paints and fluorescent fabric materials, obtained from theatrical costumiers, can be used effectively with this lamp. Do not leave the lamp on for a longer period than is necessary because it becomes very hot. It is a good idea to construct a wire screen holder.

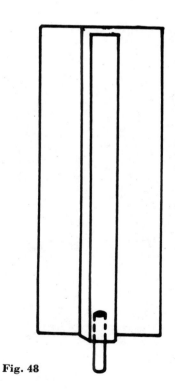

Fig. 48

75

Shadow puppets

Shadow puppets

Introduction

Shadows, besides being fascinating, contain the elements of both mystery and fantasy. People have been awed by them and amused by them. The Chinese have been using shadows as a form of theatrical entertainment for at least two thousand years and nowhere else has the shadow theatre reached such perfection. Perhaps the nearest approach exists in Indonesia, which name is so recent that the puppets of the country are still usually referred to by the old name, Javanese. There the shadow show is one of the chief forms of entertainment. India, too, has a great tradition in the shadow theatre but, as with all kinds of puppets in the countries of the East generally, the popularity of puppetry was in the entertainment it provided rather than in participation as we know it. The secrets of the art were closely guarded by the puppeteers, who handed them down through the family from generation to generation.

Undoubtedly the shadow theatre had religious significances in its beginnings and some authorities suggest that the invoking of the shadows of the ancestors had a bearing on its origin.

In the shadow theatre the 'black' shadow puppet can be adapted so that we can have coloured transparencies, which are also referred to as shadows. From the beginning the Chinese used translucent figures, which were beautifully coloured. These puppets were made from a variety of materials, including nearly transparent bone and thin strips of donkey hide or sheep skin. The Javanese or Indonesian figures are usually made of hide and embellished with the most intricate designs, achieved by piercing the leather. The figures are mounted on pointed sticks and delicately coloured and gilded. The arms are moved by control rods attached to the hands.

Shadow puppetry is not only fascinating, but practical in many uses and very stimulating to the imagination. The shadow theatre may be elaborate or simple, and the shows can be performed in a theatre, home, hospital or school with equal facility. The theatre is portable and easily stored, since practically everything can be packed flat. The puppets can be made at home without workshop facilities or elaborate tool kits.

Simple shadow figures with limited movement can be operated by young children with good effect in the dramatization of their own stories either at home or at school, where the shadow screen can also be a useful teaching aid. Hospital patients, even if confined to bed, can construct and operate shadow shows. Libraries can use them effectively in 'story hours'.

In whatever sphere it is used the shadow show will be found a versatile and satisfying medium, to which a wide variety of material can be adapted. When planning a presentation, consideration should be given to the use of narration as well as dialogue. The use of music should be carefully studied and small combinations of instruments, rather than large orchestras, are recommended.

The essentials of a shadow show are few — a translucent screen, some cut-out figures and a light. By using a large screen, human shadow plays can be given, the actors working close to the screen. The following pages contain the basic information for building a fascinating theatre of shadows.

Construction

Materials

Drawing paper

Carbon paper

Cardboard   approx. 20/1000″ thick,

for figures   small sheets
for scenery   larger sheets

Pencil and eraser

Scissors

Sharp pointed knife

Leather or paper punch (wheel type)

Paper fasteners

Bicycle spokes

Carpet warp

Coloured 'folding' or construction paper

Turpentine

Linseed oil

Black tempera paint

Brush

Figure

The shadow puppet is a two-dimensional figure and is designed by means of a line drawing.

Whether the figure is a character in a play or a variety or circus performer, the movements required from it must be known before construction begins. Furthermore, these movements should be limited to those that are absolutely essential. A shadow puppet that has every conceivable joint will need too many control wires and be extremely difficult to operate.

As a basic figure for purposes of construction, let us take a look at the outline drawing of the clown, at Fig. 49. A few details that will not show later have been drawn in for guidance.

Fig. 49   **Fig. 50**

The head and one of the arms are to be controlled. The legs are to be jointed but allowed to swing free.

The overlapping joints rotate as indicated in Fig. 50. Both solid and dotted lines should be used for clarity in the design stage. It is also well to indicate the points of attachment of the control wires, particularly if panels are to be cut for coloured transparencies. This is a precaution to ensure sufficient space being left for the wires to be jointed to the figure. The present figure will have three wires: one at the head, one on the arm, and one on the body to hold it against the screen. The legs are jointed, but are allowed free movement.

Fig. 51

The next step is to separate all the parts of the puppet, including the sections drawn in for the joints. These parts could be traced, using carbon paper, directly onto the cardboard, but an intermediate step is recommended for reasons given a little later. Trace the head of the clown through the carbon onto a sheet of clean paper. When this has been done, move the top sheet sufficiently to leave the head well clear of the traced head and then trace the body section. Continue to move the paper and trace until all the parts are shown separately, as in Fig. 51.

Next cut out all these parts; lay them one by one on the cardboard and draw around them. Remember to draw *two* arms and *two* legs.

The paper parts may now be stored in an envelope. The reason that these parts are first cut out of paper is that, should a section of the puppet be damaged at any time, the appropriate pattern could be traced on a piece of cardboard and the section quickly replaced. This storage plan would be particularly appreciated if damage was noticed just before a show.

Scissors and a sharp pointed knife are used to cut out the cardboard parts.

Now assemble the puppet, with the legs and arms placed on each side of the body. Use a needle or awl to prick through at the points to be jointed. Next, take the punch; select the right size of hole to be made and punch each piece of the cardboard separately, using the pinhole as a guide. The next step is to fasten the parts of the puppet together, using paper fasteners for the joints. Bend the points of the fasteners over carefully. Do not make the joints stiff; each limb or part of the body should move freely. It is better to have the heads of the fasteners on the side that rests against the screen to prevent the points tearing the screen material. Knotted string joints can be used instead of paper fasteners, according to preference.

If any part of a puppet or scene is taking too much strain and is liable to break, then considerable strength can be given by gluing lengths of wire to the weak parts. Always strengthen on the side of the figure away from the screen.

Shadow puppets can be made from any thin material that will not warp or 'kink' too easily. Thin sheets of zinc and plastics are readily available. The zinc will be somewhat heavy and hard to work, but very durable. If black sheet plastic, about 20/1000 of an inch, is used it will be thick enough not to warp and thin enough not to 'build up' into a figure too thick to cast a sharp-edged shadow on the screen. Wire, paper fastener or knotted string joints can be used on these figures.

Construction details of a man with guitar are shown at Fig. 52, and of a dragon at Fig. 53.

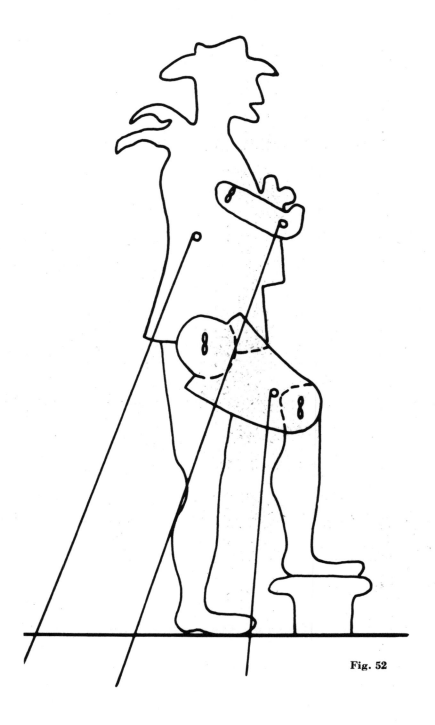

Fig. 52

Fig. 52   Shadow pattern for a guitar player

Fig. 53   Shadow pattern for a dragon

Fig. 53

Attaching the control wires

Any suitable steel wire may be used to control the puppet, but galvanized wire should be avoided because it 'kinks' easily. Bicycle spokes are as useful as anything for the controls, although they may not be long enough for some screens. Some people use umbrella ribs.

For our present purpose we shall use bicycle spokes. Take the bent end of the spoke with the small knob on it and, with a pair of pointed pliers, bend the end into a tight loop. Make two small holes at the control points already marked on the original drawing of the puppet. Pass the carpet warp through these holes and the loop on the spoke. Two or three turns should provide sufficient strength. Tie the ends of the warp at the back, but leave it sufficiently slack to enable the spoke to move freely. On no account must the spoke be rigid against the puppet.

The puppet will now appear as in Fig. 50, ready for operation. Notice that only one arm and neither of the legs is 'controlled'. However, these limbs move freely on their joints and adroit manipulation will give the effect of walking.

It is usually desirable to extend the lengths of the control wires for better operation. This is easily done by drilling and inserting the wires into lengths of wood, about ½ inch in diameter, which are then pointed at the ends as shown in Fig. 54. These wooden pieces are easier to handle than the bare wire.

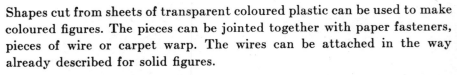

Fig. 54

Fig. 55

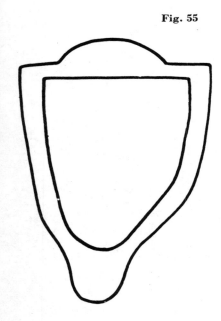

Coloured shadow puppets

Shapes cut from sheets of transparent coloured plastic can be used to make coloured figures. The pieces can be jointed together with paper fasteners, pieces of wire or carpet warp. The wires can be attached in the way already described for solid figures.

To prevent the possibility of the figures warping, the plastic used should be about 20/1000 inch thick.

These figures are manipulated in the same way as the other shadows.

Another method for making coloured puppets is to design the figures in the same manner as those given at Figs. 49 and 50.

When the various parts are cut out and ready for jointing, take a pencil and draw panels on each part, leaving an adequate frame for strength and also for the joints, as shown in Fig. 55. Cut out the panel with a sharp pointed knife.

Coloured transparent plastic or gelatine may be glued over the frames. Model aeroplane glue is best for this purpose. Plastic used for covering these panels should be considerably thinner than that used for a puppet made entirely of plastic, or the joints may be impeded.

If plastic is not available, coloured construction or folding paper may be used to obtain the colour effects. Folding paper is usually somewhat thinner than construction paper and therefore offers less resistance to light penetration. Both folding and construction paper can be made more transparent by treating it with a mixture comprising two parts linseed oil and one part turpentine. It is better to treat the paper in sheets and to cut out the necessary shapes when they are dry.

Effective coloured figures can also be constructed by making wire frames of the necessary parts and then covering them with gelatine or sheet plastic.

Coloured scenery can also be made using the principles described above.

When wire is used in the construction of both puppets and scenery, care should be taken to use a wire that will not easily bend out of shape.

Some special puppet types

If, as may well be, the same figure is required to appear on the screen from both sides during a play, construct two exactly similar puppets, but put the control wires on opposite sides.

Figures may also be constructed full face if desired, the wires being jointed at the back.

If at any time a horse and cart were required, the general construction and manipulation of the horse would be as already described. The cart would require only two wheels, which are pivoted so that they turn by contact with the operating ledge. The horse and cart could remain on the stage any length of time by means of a hinged wooden prop attached to the cart. The horse would have its separate control wires, by means of which the horse's head could be tossed every so often to keep it 'alive'. If the cart were covered, for instance, a great variety of goods, people, or both, could be unloaded from it (far more than it could possibly hold), by simply bringing any number of puppets up to the screen behind the cart and letting them off at the back.

Using the same technique, fun could be had with a patient in a dentist's chair. The dentist might remove several feet of string and other obstructions from the patient's mouth before finally producing an extra large tooth.

Shadow screens

A shadow screen may be any size, but for general use 2½' x 4' is a handy size. By careful planning, the screen can be made to fit into the opening of a glove puppet stage.

The wooden frame of the screen can be made of 1″ x 2″ lumber, with the corners joined together by 3″ flat steel angle brackets. Alternatively, artists' stretchers can be obtained in many sizes and they not only save a lot of trouble, but have a moulded front edge which gives the screen a neat appearance.

Factory cotton is a satisfactory and cheap material for the actual screen. Another excellent material is white chintz, glazed on one side. The glazed side should be at the back of the screen, because the puppets will slide easily over the shiny surface.

The screen material should be tacked as tightly as possible, but without distortion, to the frame. When this is done, thoroughly dampen the whole screen. When dry, the material will be well stretched on the frame and without wrinkles.

Unless a glove puppet stage is to be used it is now necessary to construct another frame to hold the screen. Usually this frame is of lumber, but both aluminum tubing and aluminum angle strip are very convenient alternative materials, because of their light weight. The angle strip material in particular bolts together very quickly.

The finished frame should stand upright on the floor. It should be sufficiently high so that the operator can manipulate the puppets at the bottom of the screen when standing. There should also be sufficient height for at least 12 inches of masking above the screen.

Fig. 56

The screen should now be set in the frame, at an angle of approximately 6 degrees to 8 degrees, leaning outwards at the top. See Fig. 56. This angle allows the puppets to be held closer to the screen and helps to prevent unintentional swing.

A ledge about two inches wide for the placing of properties and also to insure a constant level for the puppets should be constructed at the exact bottom edge of the screen. That means at the bottom of the 'picture' as seen from the audience. A series of holes about one inch apart should be drilled along the front of the ledge very close to the screen. It will also be found useful to have a groove running the length of the ledge. The groove will have to be very close to the holes. It could be arranged that the groove is made first and the holes bored in the groove.

The groove and holes are for the support of scenery and other effects depending on the method used for the support.

Be sure that the ledge is positioned on the operator's side of the screen, which is the side to which the material has been tacked.

Several inches below the ledge, place another considerably wider ledge to support the control wires, or extensions, when puppets are left leaning against the screen. See Fig. 57. This shelf should be covered with felt or blanketing to provide a grip for the pointed sticks or wires.

In essence, this is the complete screen and all that remains is to arrange some form of masking to conceal both the operators and the 'spill' from the lamp.

Usually this masking is arranged very much as for a hand puppet stage,

Fig. 57

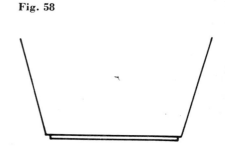

Fig. 58

with the front and sides draped and the back left open as an entrance for the manipulators. If the masking is specially arranged for the shadow theatre, depending on the size of the screen, it may be found more practicable and roomy to set the sides at more than a right angle to the front, as shown at Fig. 58. To control further light spill, it may be desirable partially to roof the booth. The roofing, of course, should be at the front, directly over the screen. The usual type of draw curtains may be installed in front of the screen, or the light may be switched off during changes of scene.

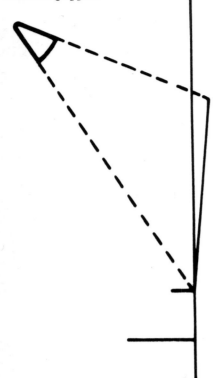

Shadow puppets

Fig. 59

Lighting the screen

It is preferable to use but one light source for the shadow screen, because of the danger of 'doubling' the shadows if more than one lamp is used.

A flood lamp will give a more even light than a spot, which tends to lose brilliance away from the centre of focus.

The actual positioning of the light for best effect usually calls for some experimenting. The light source should not be seen through the screen by the audience, so it must be either higher or lower than the screen. If it is very much higher than the top of the screen, the masking must be made high enough to contain the light. The light must also be positioned so that there is no chance that shadows from the operators' heads or arms are thrown on the screen.

Perhaps the best light position is a little above the operators' heads and a little behind their working area. Once a satisfactory light position has been established it is wise to plot this position in relation to the screen and so save the trouble of finding it each time the show is given. The approximate position of the light is shown at Fig. 59.

The light may also be thrown up or down the screen from points immediately above or below it. However, if the screen is fairly high, there would be an effect of diminishing light up or down as the case may be. Strip lighting would probably be the most effective if this method is used.

To get a sharper shadow outline from the puppets and to offset any lightening of parts of the shadow, due to the figures being slightly away from the screen at any point, paint the puppets flat black on the side that rests against the screen.

Coloured lights may be used for effect, or a sheet of coloured plastic can be placed against the screen, which will give much the same result.

Manipulation

It is fairly easy to acquire a reasonable degree of proficiency in manipulating shadow puppets. Excellent effects can be obtained with a minimum of moving parts in any one puppet. With good décor and movement of the whole puppet a very satisfactory result can be achieved. As the operator gains experience, more movement can be given to the individual figures and the actions can be made quite subtle. When they are being operated the characters should be held, but not too tightly, against the screen. If the figure is allowed to move back from the screen the shadow becomes fuzzy and less intense. For the same reason scenery should also be arranged to rest against the screen, except when less clarity of outline is desired.

The one way to learn manipulation of the shadow puppet, as with any other puppet, is to practise. The shadows will perhaps be found a little less difficult than most other puppets to get an acceptable effect, but do not be content to stop there.

Staging

Fig. 60

Scenery for the shadow play can be made in many ways.

The scene can be cut out in separate units, such as a house, a bench or a tree. See Fig. 60. Or it can be cut out of one sheet as a complete scene, as shown in Fig. 61.

If separate units are used they should have a length of wire mounted on the back of each piece. This wire extends below the bottom edge. See Fig. 62. These wires serve to stiffen the property and also enable the pieces to be 'pegged' into the holes drilled close to the screen all along the operating 'floor' already mentioned.

It takes a few seconds longer to assemble the scene in position using these separate units, but this method does allow a readjustment of the setting. Using this system the puppeteer may acquire a number of properties which can be used in various arrangements in any number of presentations.

Although unsupported scenery may be leaned against the screen without the use of the wire 'pegs', there is always the possibility of its being in-advertently moved or knocked over by a puppet while the show is in progress. The addition of the groove to the playing ledge will provide some assurance of stability for scenery not 'pegged'. The groove is also useful as a guide if anything is to move straight across the screen.

Thin sheet zinc and black plastic can also be used for scenery and effects.

Scenery can be made solid or cut out in the manner of filigree work. Paper doilies can often be employed to advantage for both costumes and scenery. Lace and semi-transparent materials can also be used effectively. These materials will be found useful for colour effects since a strong light will penetrate those of lighter weight.

Small tree branches, grasses, flowers and numerous other items from nature can be utilized in many settings.

Another and different type of scenery is the whole-sheet scene. These scenes can be prepared in black and white or in colour. For colour the scene is painted on a sheet of fairly heavy translucent paper, the size of the screen, with transparent inks or clear water colour. The sheet is then laid against the back of the screen. It would assist the smooth working of the puppets and prevent the sheet from tending to wrinkle or fall away from the screen, if a thin sheet of clear plastic were placed against it. The puppets would then have an easy, shiny surface to work on.

Black and white settings may be prepared in the same way, using opaque

Fig. 61

paint or India ink. By watering down the ink or paint slightly an illusion of distance can be created.

Another way to produce this type of scenery is to have your plain working screen removable by slotting it in your main frame structure and then change the entire screen. If the opening is to the side, the substitution of frames is a comparatively easy matter, although a front draw curtain will be necessary to conceal this operation. The cheapness of screen material makes this procedure quite practical. Extra screens are then prepared in the same way as described above for colour or black and white settings. The several scenes in a play can be changed very quickly. This is always an asset to a show. Beautiful settings for the Nativity, among other plays, can be produced and changed smoothly by this method.

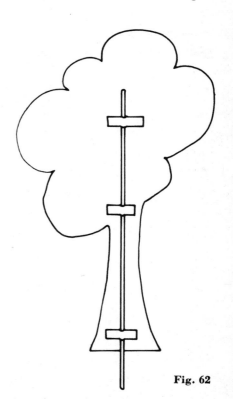

Fig. 62

Playground puppets

Playground puppets

The puppets described here are all designed to be constructed with no tools other than a pair of scissors and a knife. The materials are inexpensive and easily obtained. This makes these puppets ideally suited for playground projects, but the activity does not end with the making of the figures. It is really only the beginning, because a whole new field of interest for the young puppeteer opens up in their use.

On the following pages are given details of the construction of three types of playground puppet and suggestions as to how they may be simply, but effectively, staged. The hand and finger puppets are simplified versions of others given earlier in this book, while the third follows somewhat the lines of paper sculpture.

Materials required for construction

Construction paper	Plasticine
Cardboard	Parcel string
Crêpe paper (in several colours)	Lollipop sticks
Asbestos powder	Poster paint and brushes
French chalk	A small can of glue
Cold water paste powder	

Sheets of paper, for the papier-mâché overcast method (see page 28).

With these materials and a knife and scissors, all the puppets described here can be made, as can also some effective properties with which to stage them attractively.

Hand puppet with papier-mâché head

Head

Form some plasticine into a ball about 2–2½ inches in diameter. Roll another piece of plasticine to the thickness and about half the length of the forefinger. Join the roll to the ball as shown in Fig. 63. Cover the head with layers of paper as described for the overcast papier-mâché method on Page 28. When the head is dry, cut it open and remove the plasticine. Join the halves again by pasting strips of ordinary wrapping paper over the crack and allow to dry thoroughly.

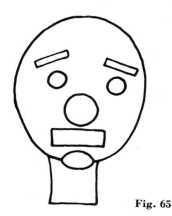

Fig. 63

Features

The features may be formed by applying to the head a series of simple basic shapes, shown at Fig. 64, made with the asbestos modelling composition described on Page 32.

Roll two small balls for the eyes.

Roll a larger ball for the nose.

Two thin rolls make the eyebrows.

The chin begins as another small ball, flattened on one side.

The lips can be formed from two short rolls.

The lips can be replaced by an oblong piece which can be shaped into a moustache.

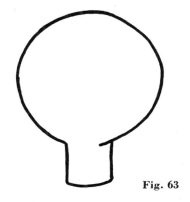

Fig. 64

Now that the shapes are all ready, take a look at Fig. 65 to see how they are placed in position to form a face on one side of the round head.

Put a little paste on the head at the points where you are going to place the nose and the eyes.

Place the three balls in position and flatten them slightly.

Now set the two thin rolls just above each eye in the position of the eyebrows. Flatten these slightly also.

Take the flat-sided ball you have for the chin and put that in position at the bottom of the face. Use some more of the composition and model it to become part of the face.

To form the lips, place the two remaining rolls between the nose and the chin and push them gently until they are well joined to the face.

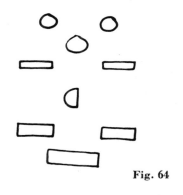

Fig. 65

97

Fig. 66

Finishing the head

With the fingers, or a piece of flat wood such as a tongue depressor, work on these features until they look the way you want them. A little touch here and there can do a great deal to change the whole character of the face. See Fig. 66.

If your character requires a moustache, then, if you wish, you can dispense with the lips and use instead the oblong shape you still have left. This can be shaped in a variety of ways, according to character. A suggestion of hair can be given to the moustache by scoring it with the knife blade.

Now make the ears from two more rolls of the modelling composition. Curve the rolls and press them in position on either side of the head. Make sure that the front of the ears merge into the side of the head.

The main part of the head is now done and must be left in a warm spot until completely dry.

The hair can be made of string or strips of paper pasted on the head. Wool or scraps of fur can also be used for both the hair and the moustache. However, it is better to wait until the head is painted before using either fur or wool.

Hands

The hands may be made while the head is drying.

Form two balls of the modelling composition which, in relation to the puppet head, are about the size of a closed fist.

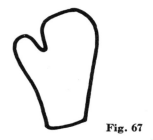

Fig. 67

Roll these balls out slightly and flatten them a little. Now they may be easily and quickly shaped into the puppet's hands (one right and one left), with only the thumb separated from the main part of the hand, as shown in Fig. 67. Fig. 68 shows the fingers in a bent position.

Leave the hand shapes to dry and then mount them into the ends of two cardboard tubes, made to fit the puppeteer's thumb and little finger respectively. Use some paste and a little of the composition to fill the space between the hand and the tube.

Painting the puppet

Fig. 68

When the head and hands are thoroughly dry, paint them with poster colours. White with yellow and a touch of red makes a suitable flesh colour. Add a brown to darken if necessary. A little fleck of white on the pupils of the eyes after they are painted helps to give them a 'live' look. Paint the arms and hands flesh colour and indicate the fingers with brownish lines.

Dressing the puppet

The puppet can be dressed in a crêpe paper or cloth costume. The general shape of the costume will be the same as that given on Page 42, only smaller. Do not make the costume too short or the puppeteer's arm will be seen during the show.

If preferred, the puppet may be 'costumed' by merely draping the hand with a handkerchief, or pushing the index finger up through a hole in a piece of material and placing the head on the protruding finger without attaching it permanently to the costume.

Accessories, such as a pair of spectacles, can easily be made from a length of wire.

Paper sculpture hand puppet

White cardboard or construction paper is best for making this quick project puppet.

With a little ingenuity and imagination some surprisingly good results can be obtained.

The shape of the face, eyes, ears and the mouth can all be changed to give the head a variety of characteristics. The hair style will also do a great deal to change the character. For instance, coloured construction paper cut to represent feathers will help make an Indian look convincing.

Use the patterns given at Fig. 69 as basic designs on which to build a number of different characters.

Remember that each head has two eyes and two ears and, of course, you will also need two hands.

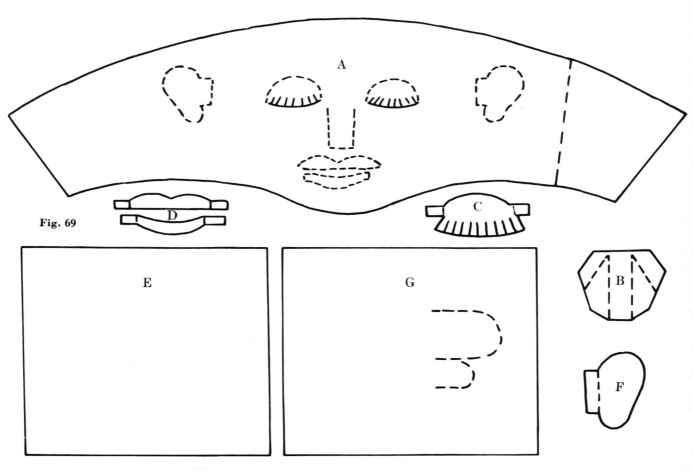

Fig. 69

To begin with, trace the patterns on to thick cardboard. Cut them out and use as master patterns.

Now trace each individual section of the pattern on to the cardboard or construction paper that is to be used for the head.

Cut these pieces out and remember to make two each of the eyes, ears and hands.

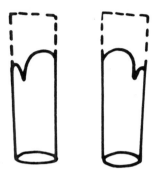

Fig. 70

Assembling the head

Bend piece (A) (head) and glue the overlap together at the dotted line.

Fold the nose (B) along the dotted lines. The two outer segments fold under and are glued to the face in the position shown at Fig. 69.

Cut along the lines on the two eye pieces (C) to form the eyelashes.

Bend the flaps back at the end of the eyes and glue to the head in the position indicated at Fig. 69. Do not press the eye flat to the head, but maintain its shape. The lashes may be bent up a bit.

The mouth (D) is in two sections. Bend and glue the tabs in the position indicated. Treat the mouth like the eyes and maintain the shape.

The piece marked (E) is the neck and this should be rolled around the forefinger to the correct size. Glue down the overlapping portion. If the overlap is too great, cut off the excess length. When the glue on the neck is dry, use more glue to stick it to the inside of the back of the head. Make sure the neck piece extends well below the head.

The ears (F) may be glued to the sides of the head as soon as the neck is in position and dry.

Except for the hair, the head is complete. Curled paper glued to the inside edge of the head makes good hair. If desired, a top may be put on the head and hair of any suitable material glued to it.

Fig. 71

To make the hands, roll one pattern (G) around the little finger and glue the overlap. Roll the second pattern (G) around the thumb and glue the overlap in the same way.

Flatten both rolls of cardboard at the ends that have the hands indicated on them. Glue these ends down to a point that includes the shape of the hands. When dry cut out the hands as shown in Fig. 70.

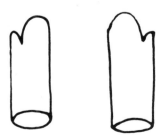

Fig. 71 shows the head and hands ready to paint. Use poster colours for painting the head and hands. The pupils of the eyes should be painted on the face under the eyelids.

The puppet can be dressed very simply in material or crêpe paper, using the general principles suggested for the papier-mâché hand puppet previously described in this section.

Playground finger puppet

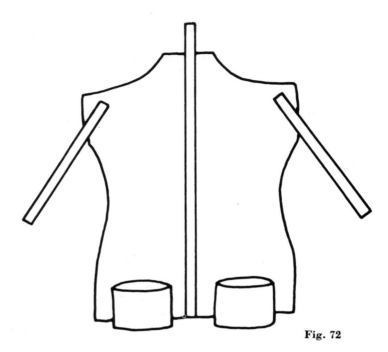

Fig. 72

This is another version of the finger puppet described earlier in this book at Page 66, but it is greatly simplified and designed to be constructed from materials usually found on the playground. As with the other finger puppets, the first and second fingers of the operator's hand act as the legs. By movement of the fingers the figure will walk about quite freely and convincingly. The length of the puppet's legs is automatically decided by the length of the operator's fingers.

Body

Two short tubes of cardboard should be made to fit in the ring positions of the first and second fingers.

A flat body shape, from hips to shoulders, Fig. 72, is also cut out of cardboard.

The two tubes are glued on each side of the lower part, as shown in Fig. 72.

A lollipop stick, or similar piece of wood, is glued on the back of the body with half an inch left protruding at the neck. This serves both as a stiffener for the body and as a point upon which to mount the head.

Arms may be made by gluing to the shoulders two lollipop or large match sticks, cut to the right lengths (Fig. 72), but more flexibility is obtained by using two pieces of string.

102

Using the modelling compound, model the hands on the ends of the sticks or string. If string is used tie a small knot at the lower end to provide a grip for the compound.

Head

The easiest way to provide a head for this type of puppet is to roll some modelling compound into a ball, not more than 1¼ inches in diameter, and then, when dry, simply paint all the features on it. If desired, the nose and ears can be modelled on. This will be more effective.

While the head is still soft, place it over the wood that is left sticking up above the shoulders and move it around a little, until it fits quite easily. It is not necessary to fix the head to the neck. If left free, it will have a slight movement when the puppet is operated.

Paint the head and hands with poster paints, but do not varnish. A shiny surface picks up lights and the features will, to a great extent, be lost.

The hair can be paper, string, wool or may be modelled on with the compound.

Costume

A suitable costume can be made from coloured crêpe paper, which does not tear too easily. Cloth materials can, of course, be used if they are available. The costume can be glued to the body, but trousers or a skirt should be carried around the cardboard rings through which the fingers are placed to operate the puppet.

The fingers are also effective as bare legs. Small fingertip shoes can be made, using the modelling compound. Make the sole of the shoe on the shorter finger a little thicker in order to compensate for the difference in length of the fingers.

Manipulation

Since these puppets are only simplified versions of the Hand Puppets and Finger Puppets described earlier at Pages 6 and 66, it is recommended that the same general principles be followed regarding their manipulation. It will be found just as easy to handle properties with these simple hand puppets as with the more elaborate varieties, but the properties should be made of light-weight materials.

Most of the standard puppet plays can be adapted for use with these puppets, or scripts can be written specially for them. This is always a good idea because it is excellent practice and everything can be adjusted in regard to the limitations of the playground.

A stage for finger puppets

A large cardboard carton can be adapted to form an effective stage for the Finger puppets. Fig. 73 shows how the carton is cut to make a one-piece stage.

(A) is the opening through which the audience sees the puppets. A suggested size for the opening is 8″ x 24″, although it may be any size to suit the particular requirements.

(B) is the front masking that conceals at least part of the operators from the audience.

(C) is the background, which can be about 10 inches high.

(D) and (E) are made from pieces of the carton that were cut out when the stage was made. These are the wings that conceal the puppets before they appear. Make these tabs about 4 inches wide and the same height as the background.

The stage depth will, of course, depend on the size of the carton.

The stage can be placed on a large box or a low table, according to the size of the operators. If a table is used, it could be masked around with brown paper or other suitable material.

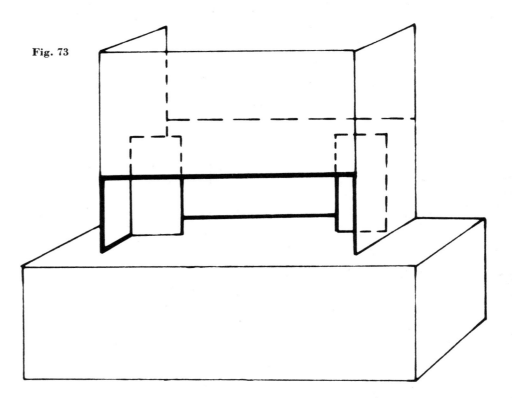

Fig. 73

If possible, the operator's hands should be covered with black material, such as an old stocking or glove. If this is done, then the whole of the inside of the stage should be painted a flat black. Tempera colour will do very well.

The two wings can be made removable. If scenery is sometimes to be used, they can be replaced with other wings that fit in with the required scene.

Because the hand and arm is covered with black material, care should be taken when using scenery, as a part of it will always be blotted out when puppets are on the stage. Flat cut-out pieces, such as trees or a house, will be most effective and they can be pinned to the background.

Properties such as chairs, tables or other furniture can be made from thick cardboard and painted. Be sure you keep these to a minimum or there will be no room to move on the stage.

Playground presentation

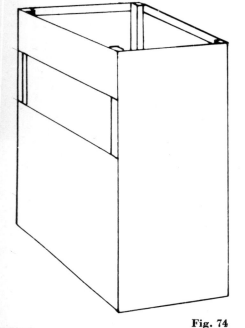

Fig. 74

A box stage

Fig. 74 shows how a refrigerator-carton can be made into a simple box stage for hand puppets.

An opening cut in the top half of one side becomes the proscenium through which the puppets are seen by the audience.

A larger opening is cut in the back of the carton to form an entrance for the performers. This opening should start a few inches above the ground and finish just below the level of the front opening. In this way light entering the back will not show through the back-cloth, which should be hung about nine inches behind the proscenium opening and reaching down to an inch or two below it. If the light were not shut off in this way, the puppeteers' heads would be seen by the audience in silhouette behind the back-cloth.

The back-cloth should be of a fine material that allows the operators to see out, but prevents the audience from seeing through. If theatrical gauze (scrim) is used — and it is cheap — scenes can be painted on it with tempera paint.

If preferred, the front opening can be cut nearer the top of the carton, above the head level of the operators, who could then manipulate above their heads instead of looking through the back-drop. This method allows the top half of the back of the stage to be used as a background and for scenery.

An open stage

Fig. 75 shows another way to stage these puppets. This is a very simple method which can be used either indoors or out.

A table, or anything handy that will form a partition about four feet long and two feet six inches high, may be draped with paper or other material.

This is then placed parallel with a wall or fence and about two feet away from it. The operators sit or crouch behind the table or partition and work with the puppets along its back edge. The wall or fence acts as a background, to which may be fastened flat cut-out scenic effects.

The alcove formed by draping a table makes a good storage place for the puppets and properties.

Fig. 75

If used in the open, the scene effects could be mounted on pointed sticks, which are then stuck into the ground. This method quickens up scene changes and also allows scenery 'in depth'.

Flat cut-out tree

Cut out several shapes from construction paper to represent foliage.

Cut out the shape of the tree-trunk and glue the pieces of foliage to the top of it so that they overlap each other, as shown in Fig. 76. Cut the tree-trunk the full height of the tree, including the foliage, and it will then serve as a strengthener when the foliage is glued to it.

If a tree, or any other section of the scenery, is required to be of a more permanent nature, cut the parts out of thick card.

Paint the properties and scenic effects with poster paint, but do not leave them in the open after use for they will spoil if it rains.

Fig. 76

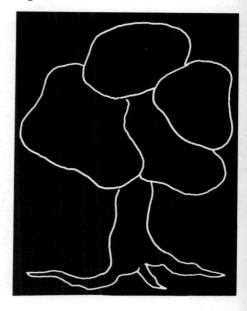

Plays

Think!

Because your physical self is hidden when you are manipulating puppets, do not for one second imagine that the audience cannot both 'see' your expression and 'read' your mind. In other words, if, when holding a puppet on stage, you are taking things easy or thinking about something else and only just remembering your cues in time as the dialogue pours off a tape, or is being voiced 'off stage', your mental state inevitably carries through to the audience, who quickly become bored. The words 'holding a puppet' are used advisedly because, under these circumstances, that is all you are doing with it.

It is absolutely essential to THINK from the beginning to the end of the show — to be as aware of the audience as you would be if you were on stage yourself. Nothing calls for more constant thought and alertness than does a theatrical performance.

Voicing of the puppet by the manipulator tends to keep the attention from wandering from the show, but this also entails thinking about two things at once. Quite often, concentration on the lines results in less concentration on the puppet. This means that it is necessary to be word-perfect in order to act convincingly the roles dictated by the dialogue.

No criticism is being levelled at any of the voice methods mentioned above. Inevitably you must use one of them. However, 'remote' voice does perhaps tend to lull the manipulator into a false sense of being only half the show, with correspondingly less effort required. Less control at one end should mean greater alertness at the other, particularly when the voices are live and the speed and emphasis is apt to vary at times.

After the condemnation, what is to be done?

As with most things, correction is largely a matter of practice. It is clear that to practise thinking it is necessary to have something to think about. If your show does not provide you with thinking material, you have no show! If you are not thinking you cannot act, and if you are not acting, you are better doing something else. Thinking and acting are full-time jobs during the show and if you concentrate on acting with your puppet, your own interest is kept high. Enthusiasm reaches the audience as surely as does apathy. And do not think for a moment that acting with a puppet is any less exacting than human acting. In many respects it is more exacting, since the possible movements for the puppet are more limited.

Examine your material carefully and decide whether it is really suitable. When you are satisfied that it is, become thoroughly familiar with the lines, not only of the parts that involve you directly, but also of every other part in the play, whether you are on stage or not. Your interpretation must be in tune with the whole; otherwise the presentation will be uneven. A director for the production will help to correct this, but his or her job will be easier if everyone knows every part.

Your acting should be sustained whether or not your puppet is speaking, or when other characters have the centre stage. This demands a great deal of thinking since your movements then are reactions and are no longer declamatory. Remember that the puppet characters are still in view of the audience whether they are speaking or not. They must at all times be a live part of the performance.

Practise the art of pantomime, using both broad and subtle movements. Where possible act out parts of the play without the words. This will also assist you in those parts where you have periods on stage without speaking. Do not spend this time jogging around aimlessly — it only distracts the attention of the audience.

Another aid to thinking when manipulating a puppet is the interpretation of music into movement. Do not choose a fast piece of music, but something fairly slow and 'moody'. Listen to it a few times and then translate your reactions into puppet movements. This will *make* you think. It will help to smooth out jerkiness from your puppet movements generally and also stimulate another means of expression. A wider variety of means of expressing yourself through your puppets will help to keep high your own interest and therefore that of your audience. You owe this to them. Remember at all times that the audience rightly expects to be entertained, not to be the innocent victims of your moods.

These suggestions will help to keep you on your toes and keep you thinking during a performance, but nothing is a cure-all. You, yourself, are the most important factor in any prescription.

A play for puppets in two acts **The boy with green fingers**

by Elizabeth Merten

Characters:

Mistress Jones

Gary 'Greenfingers' Jones   A young boy (about ten years old, with red hair, green eyes and green-painted hands)

A witch

Master Potts   An old gardener

A Sergeant

A Corporal

A Princess

Scene   The interior of a country cottage.

Act. I — rather dim and shadowy lighting with an effect of firelight if possible; in this act there is a cradle on stage.

Act II — bright lighting, giving an effect of sunlight. The set has two windows with tall flowers growing outside; there is a table with a bowl of flowers in the room.

Properties   A cradle

A table, with a bowl of flowers and an open book on it

A scroll

A flower-pot containing a plant

Music   Folk-tunes, for opening, entr'acte and closing

15 minutes   two manipulators

113

Production notes

These notes are not intended to dictate the exact way the play should be produced, but are included as a guide to the various possibilities and the treatments that could be used. Every producer should bring as much individuality as possible to a production.

The play was written for hand puppets, but a stronger impact will be obtained in Act I if the witch is a hand and rod puppet. Before the witch actually appears on the stage, she can be given an effective build-up by lighting and shadows, and by suitable music; when she appears she can have long arms and flowing draperies. This will help create a feeling of impending evil and the witch's pronouncements will be all the more effective, particularly if the voice is well cast. This treatment would also strengthen the character, who, by casting a spell, provides the whole basis for the plot, but has only one brief appearance.

The characters

The Witch, as already suggested, would be more striking if she is a hand and rod puppet. The head modelling should be strong and well defined. Be careful not to reduce the strength of the features when painting the head. Remember this character appears only in a faintly-lit room. Make the under-glove and the flowing draperies of the costume exceptionally long, so that the figure can appear to fly rather than walk. The hand control wires should be correspondingly long.

The Baby is not seen, and only heard briefly, in Act I; being tucked up in the depths of the cradle.

Mistress Jones should be a normally pleasant character dressed in the story-book costume of a country woman, with, perhaps, a mob cap.

Mr. Potts is a kindly old man with a weatherbeaten face and white hair. Such accessories as spectacles or a moustache could be considered. Some part of his costume could be a faded green colour.

Gary 'Greenfingers' Jones is described in the play as 'ugly'. This should be an appealing ugliness, not the repulsive type. Considerable care should be given to achieving this effect since he is the chief character in the play.

The two Soldiers should be in typical toy-soldier costumes, with three and two stripes respectively.

The Princess is young and beautiful and dressed in pink or blue, as story-book princesses invariably are.

The full effect of the setting will depend largely on the type of stage used. If the background is painted on a scrim, then it is merely a question of showing two windows with perhaps a dresser and chair also painted in. The cradle can be clipped to the back edge of the playboard. However, some consideration should be given, in addition to the replacing of the cradle by a table in Act II, to the passing of ten years. This could be effected by a quick change of scrims during the brief curtain between the acts. (This interval should be counted in seconds, not minutes!) The scrim for the opening scene could, for instance, have closed shuttered windows and other characteristics that would assist in the creation of the desired atmosphere.

The general lighting should be dim, as though from an oil lamp, but there should be sufficient light in which to play the scene without appreciably increasing it after Mistress Jones' entrance.

The scrim for Act II would have the windows in exactly the same positions as for the opening scene, but they would be open to bright sunlight with tall flowers growing outside.

The bowl of flowers should be fastened to the table. This makes one instead of two properties to position in a short space of time and also eliminates the possibility of the bowl being knocked over or displaced.

If desired, the backgrounds could be merely 'draped', in which case it would be more effective to use two different colours of scrim type material that could be changed in the way suggested above. This treatment would give a distinct change of atmosphere and time to the two scenes. A dark blue or dark grey for the first act and either a medium grey or soft light brown for Act II would be suitable.

If the play is to be given on a stage where the puppets are held higher than the operator's head then the setting should be designed to the full depth of the stage. One or two wing drapes, or tabs, will give the witch more scope for movement. She might flit from one tab to another and peer around before finally approaching the cradle and uttering the fateful curse.

With this type of stage two added effects could be gained if the garden scene were set back nine to twelve inches behind the window set. This could also effect an economy in the setting as the windows could have movable shutters which could be closed during the first act and opened on the pre-set garden scene for the second act. The lighting here would also be effective if it were dim behind the shuttered windows and increased to bright sunlight in the second act. An effect might also be gained by some movement of the closed shutters prior to the entrance of the witch.

The soldiers and the princess could be made to pass by the windows before entering. If you do this, remember they should pass by again after their exits.

The boy with green fingers

If the stage area is large enough, consideration might be given to the use of a well-ballasted pedestal that reaches to the eye-level of the playboard. Both the cradle and the table could be clipped to this in turn. More effects can be gained if the puppets can move all round these properties.

Whatever treatment and colour schemes are involved in the production, work all this out before designing the costumes. The characters must always stand out from the backgrounds, not be overwhelmed by them. In a well-balanced stage design the characters and backgrounds should complement each other and, with careful study beforehand, the colours used can become as integral a part of the presentation as can music, for instance. This does not mean that the colours used should 'match'; violent clashes of the right colours can greatly assist the dramatic effects if they are the *right* colours. Do not neglect the possibility of dyeing materials if you cannot buy the colours suitable for your purpose.

G. M.

The Boy With Green Fingers

Act one

[*As curtain opens, Witch enters from stage left, looks around and creeps in a sinister fashion across stage towards cradle, cackling as she goes.*]

WITCH: Ah-hah! A new baby, I see! Nobody watching it either — here's a chance for me. Ha-ha! Nothing I enjoy so much as casting a spell over a new baby! [*She cackles and crouches over cradle.*] May you be so stupid and ugly that everyone will laugh and be unkind to you all your miserable life! [*She laughs in a cracked voice and gloats over the cradle. The baby cries.*]

[*Mrs. Jones enters from stage left, sees the witch and screams in horror.*]

WITCH: [*triumphantly*] The spell is cast. Too late! Too late!

[*She cackles as she flies off and exits stage right.*]

MRS. JONES: Oh, my poor baby! What has that dreadful witch done to you? Oh dear, what shall I do? Your life will be ruined from the start, if I can't find some way of breaking the spell. Oh dear! Oh dear!

[*Master Potts, the old gardener, enters from stage right. He peers at Mrs. Jones.*]

POTTS: You sound terrible upset, Mistress Jones — what's the matter?

MRS. JONES: Oh, Master Potts, I heard the baby cry just now and when I came into the room I saw a horrible witch bending over the cradle. She flew away as fast as lightning, but she had already laid a wicked spell on my son. [*Mrs. Jones sobs.*]

POTTS: Dear me, that's very serious, to be sure. Now let me think what's to be done. [*He scratches his head and thinks for a moment.*] I'm only an old gardener, of more use to the flowers than to human beings . . . but there's one thing I can do for him. May I touch the baby, Mistress Jones, just for a moment? You know I wouldn't hurt the little fellow.

MRS. JONES: Yes, yes, do anything that might help to break the spell . . . what are you going to do?

[*Master Potts crosses to cradle and touches the baby. He then stands up straight and speaks proudly.*]

POTTS: Now come and look at your child.

MRS. JONES: [*going to cradle and bending over*] Master Potts! What have you done, you stupid old man? What's that green stuff on his hands . . . as though things weren't bad enough already. Take it off this instant . . . hurry, you idiot!

POTTS: [*hurt but dignified*] So you don't appreciate my gift to the baby! Don't you know what having green fingers means?

MRS. JONES: Whoever heard of such a thing? Take it off at once.

POTTS: Once the gift of green fingers is given, it can never be taken back again.

MRS. JONES: [*horrified*] What?

POTTS: You don't understand . . . it means that your son will have a power over plants and flowers that will seem like magic . . . nothing will ever fail to grow for him.

MRS. JONES: Well, that's a great consolation, I must say.

POTTS: I thought it might be something to make the poor boy happy — just to be able to grow lovely flowers. If he is going to have other unpleasant things to face in his life, just think of the pleasure of looking at a perfect rose.

MRS. JONES: Perfect fiddlesticks! Now my poor child has to go through life with goodness knows what evils dogging his footsteps — and green fingers besides! If that's all you can do, Master Potts, go away at once and never come into this cottage again.

[*She turns her back on him.*]

POTTS: [*angrily*] And not a word of thanks! Oh well, you'll see, you ungrateful woman. One day when I am dead and gone you will wish you had said a thank-you to this crazy old man. Just you wait and see.

[*Mrs. Jones laughs scornfully, still with her back to him.*]

POTTS: You wait and see.

[*Master Potts exits stage right. Mrs. Jones turns and bends over the cradle again as the curtain closes and music begins.*]

Act two

[*As music fades and curtain opens, Gary "Greenfingers" Jones, a boy of ten, is at a table looking at a book. A bowl of flowers on the table attracts his attention and he touches the flowers gently. Mrs. Jones enters from stage right in time to see the gesture.*]

MRS. JONES: Gary! Get on with your lessons. What page are you at now?

GARY: Page one.

MRS. JONES: That's disgraceful — you're a lazy and useless boy. Read me the first sentence at the top of page two.

GARY: [*haltingly*] The boy — said — I wish — I was — in the garden — where — the grass is green — and soft — and — the sun —

MRS. JONES: [*interrupting*] Gary! You're making that up. It's not in the book at all, you bad boy.

[*Gary shakes with laughter.*]

MRS. JONES: No, it's not funny, Gary. Read me what is there, if you please, and stop plaguing your poor widowed mother.

GARY: [*sighing deeply*] But I'm only interested in flowers, not in books. What's the use of having green fingers if you won't let me use them?

MRS. JONES: I'm waiting . . . Oh, how I wish that Master Potts had kept his gift to himself.

GARY: [*sighing again*] The cat — sat — on the . . .

MRS. JONES: [*looking out of the window*] Gracious me, there's a great big carriage outside and a soldier coming up the path. I wonder what he wants?

[*Gary turns and goes to look too. He becomes excited.*]

GARY: Isn't it exciting, mother?

[*A sergeant enters from stage left, carrying in his hands an opened scroll, from which he reads.*]

SERGEANT: Silence, good people all, and listen to the Royal Pronouncement.

[*Gary and Mrs. Jones bow and stand close together, listening.*]

SERGEANT: Somewhere in this village there is known to be a young male person who is said to be very ugly and stupid.

[*Gary and Mrs. Jones turn and look at each other, then listen again.*]

SERGEANT: He is quite small and has red hair and green eyes. He is a very bad scholar and has a mischievous character.

[*Gary hides behind Mrs. Jones and as the following speech finishes he makes for the exit stage right.*]

SERGEANT: All good citizens are required to assist in the finding of this person and the search will continue until he is found, by order of His Majesty.

[*He stops reading and spots Gary, about to disappear.*]

119

SERGEANT: Hey! come back here . . . where d'you think you're going? [*He takes a good look at Gary.*] Well, what d'you know — just a minute now. [*He pulls Gary back to centre-stage.*] Red hair, green eyes . . . ugly . . . h'm, h'm . . . and green fingers too! I'm blest if you're not the very one we're looking for.

MRS. JONES: [*very agitated*] Oh, sir, he's my only son. What has he done? He is indeed ugly and stupid and mischievous . . . but he's all I've got, General.

SERGEANT: [*clearing his throat*] Er, h'm — not a general yet, madam, just a sergeant.

MRS. JONES: And a very fine one you look too.

SERGEANT: Thank you, madam.

MRS. JONES: Please may I speak to my son before you take him away?

SERGEANT: Oh well, I don't see any harm in that, but don't be long now.

MRS. JONES: What have you been up to, Gary?

GARY: N-n-nothing, mother . . . nothing at all. There must be a mistake.

MRS. JONES: There must be a mistake, Sergeant.

SERGEANT: I don't think so, madam, but we can soon find out. [*Shouts in his army voice.*] Corporal!

[*They all look towards off-stage left. Corporal enters, bearing a flower-pot with the top of a very sorry-looking plant showing in it.*]

SERGEANT: [*to Gary*] Now then, my lad. We, that is, the Royal Family and myself, have been hearing some remarkable things about you. This extremely rare foreign plant [*he gestures towards the Corporal*] is the pride and joy of the Crown Princess and, as you can see, it is withering away. All the — hrmphm, hrmphm — horti- horti- horticultural experts — [*aside*] that means the best gardeners, I suppose — have tried in vain to revive it, and the Princess is very upset and worried. In fact, I declare she is fading away too. So here's your chance, my boy — if you really have the powers we've heard about, give this plant a new lease of life and your fortune will be made. If you can't . . . well, let me see . . . p'raps you'd make a good soldier . . . yes, if you fail, we'll recruit you for the army.

MRS. JONES: Oh no . . . please don't take him away.

SERGEANT: Now then, Corporal — three paces forward M-A-R-R-CH! Halt! Now then, Master Gary Greenfingers — it's up to you. Proceed.

120

[*Gary approaches the pot and strokes the plant.*]

GARY: [*softly*] Poor plant . . . poor lonely plant . . . far away from your own country . . . you just need a little affection, don't you . . .

[*Slowly the plant rises above the level of the rim of the pot and blossoms appear on the stalk. It should rise a good way above the head of the Corporal. Gary shows it to the Sergeant and moves closer to his mother again. The Sergeant comes forward and inspects it closely.*]

SERGEANT: [*in wonder*] Well, if I hadn't seen that happen, I wouldn't have believed it. That's the most wonderful thing I ever saw . . . now you will be rewarded for your cleverness. Just wait till the Princess sees it. Take it out to the carriage, Corporal, and show it to Her Highness.

[*The Corporal carries the plant out stage left.*]

MRS. JONES: [*excitedly*] The Princess is here? [*Gary turns and looks out of the window.*]

GARY: Oh, mother, isn't it thrilling — we'll never forget this day, shall we?

SERGEANT: [*roaring*] Attention, everyone.

[*All stand stock still. The Princess enters from stage left. She is young and beautiful.*]

PRINCESS: Where is the person who gave my plant back its life and beauty?

SERGEANT: [*to Gary*] Three paces forward — MARCH.

PRINCESS: [*extending a hand, as Gary bows*] We are proud to have you among our subjects. There are few with such a wonderful gift as yours. I appoint you here and now Head Gardener to the Palace for the rest of your life.

[*Mrs. Jones gasps for joy.*]

GARY: I can never thank you enough, Your Highness.

PRINCESS: Is this your mother?

MRS. JONES: Welcome to our humble cottage, Your Highness. Your presence is a very great honour for us, Your Highness.

PRINCESS: Your home may be humble, but all these flowers make it a place of beauty. You must be proud of your clever son.

MRS. JONES: Indeed I am, Your Highness.

PRINCESS: Fare you well then, but see that he arrives at the Palace early tomorrow to take over his duties.

121

[*Gary and Mrs. Jones bow low as the Princess exits stage left, followed by the Sergeant.*]

MRS. JONES: Gary Greenfingers Jones, you wonderful, clever, darling boy.

GARY: Hurray, hurray!

[*They hug each other, then Mrs. Jones looks at Gary seriously.*]

MRS. JONES: But there's one thing we must not forget, Gary.

[*He nods in agreement and they turn to the front, raise their faces skywards and say very solemnly in unison.*]

GARY AND MRS. JONES: [*together*] Thank you, Master Potts.

[*As curtain closes, soft folk-tune concludes the show.*]

A play for hand puppets **A head for Peppino**

by George Merten

Characters:

Peppino   A boy puppet with red hair and a longish, uptilted nose and bright eyes. The head is not fastened to the costume, but may be removed as necessary from the forefinger to allow the substitution of other heads.

Peppino has two extra heads — a dog's head and a cannibal's head with a bone through the nose. Both heads have bright red hair.

Magician   Dressed in traditional robes, but not a frightening character. He has a domed forehead, is benevolent and somewhat absent-minded.

Blinkie   A clown

A narrator reads the prologue

Scene   This play can very well be done in drapes, but if scenery is desired then it could be set in either a puppet workshop or back stage in a hand puppet theatre.

Properties   A stage mirror, a light screen, large enough to conceal a puppet adequately.

about 15 minutes   two or three manipulators

Production notes

Two things in particular are of extreme importance to the success of this play — the timing and an imaginative voice for the Magician. There is ample scope for pantomime and for good acting generally. It will be found effective if the narration is given over very soft background music, but the music will need to be chosen with great care because at no point must it predominate. To this end the music should maintain a fairly constant level of sound and should be faded as the curtain opens. Study the play carefully, particularly with regard to the timing of the entrances and exits during the spell sequences. Once Peppino has appeared wearing in turn each of the two extra heads, it is unnecessary to use the puppet body when these heads appear round the side of the screen, either separately or together.

The play can be given with two manipulators, but three will enable more character to be given to each role. In any case, considerable rehearsal will be necessary to effect a smooth flow of movement.

The characters

All three puppets should have as long arms as possible, but still retain the ability to handle the properties as necessary. Felt covered wire hands are recommended.

Peppino should be quite amusing, but also attractive. His hair should be as red as possible. For the best effect, theatrical crêpe hair is suggested.

Take care that all three heads fit snugly on the finger, otherwise they may drop off at the wrong moment.

It is not essential that his nose should be long, but it will assist to make the character amusing, but not necessarily ugly.

The red hair should be a distinctive feature of the other two heads since this provides the common denominator.

Great care should be taken that the Magician is an amiable character, both in appearance and manner. His robes could be decorated with the usual symbols associated with magicians, but avoid anything of a frightening nature, otherwise the character will be inconsistent with the magician of the play. No mention is made of a wand, but one may be used if desired.

Blinkie is an ordinary circus clown. If his eyes are crossed with a plus (+) sign, it will assist to point up his name. Care should be taken that no part of his costume impedes his handling of the properties.

124

The setting

Drapes are suggested as the background for the play, but be careful to make the drape and costume colours complementary. The puppets should not be absorbed by the background. In planning this, take into account the extra heads to be used in the play.

The properties

There are only two properties other than the extra heads — the mirror and the screen. The mirror should not be a real mirror (that would be contrary to theatrical tradition), but a painted mirror set up on a firm, flat base. The mirror itself is never seen by the audience. The screen must be of light-weight material because the clown has to hold it up for quite a long time. It can have some suitable design painted on it, but this should not be over-elaborate, otherwise it will detract from the heads that are poked out from it. It must be large enough to conceal Peppino and also the manipulator's two hands when the heads are used separately from the body.

Lighting

The lighting will be more effective if dimmers are available. White light, with perhaps some pink or blue added to tone it down in brightness, will create more 'atmosphere'. The lights should fade with the drawing of the final curtain.

G. M.

A head for Peppino

NARRATOR: Peppino is a puppet. He hasn't been a puppet very long because the puppet-maker has only just finished him. Peppino has spent most of his life so far hanging upside down on a hook beside some other puppets. Peppino noticed that no two of the puppets looked the same and this caused him to wonder what *he* looked like. Towards the end of Peppino's first day a young girl, whom the puppet-maker called 'daughter', came to look at him. Of course, Peppino didn't know she was a young girl, but he did wonder why she was able to move about by herself, just like the puppet-maker. 'Daughter' took Peppino off his hook and laughed as she said, 'What a funny face you have, Peppino.' Then she laughed louder still. For some reason this hurt Peppino and he began to dislike his face, even though he had never seen it. Not long after this the lights went out and 'daughter' and the puppet-maker went away and all was quiet. Peppino was still thinking about his face when he heard a voice near him say, 'They have gone; we can do what we like now.' Peppino heard some shuffling sounds as it gradually began to get light again. He then saw that some of the puppets were now up the other way. While trying to see what they were doing Peppino found that he could move quite easily, so he crept over quietly and peeped at the puppets from behind a curtain.

[*Curtain up shows the Magician and the Clown on stage with Peppino peeping around the curtain at stage left.*]

BLINKIE: I wonder what the master is going to do with the new one?

MAGICIAN: Perhaps he is going to do something different. I must remember to look in my crystal ball.

[*He looks in Peppino's direction and nearly catches him, but Peppino dodges back just in time.*]

BLINKIE: Then he will be laying us aside and . . .

MAGICIAN: [*interrupting*] You don't have to worry; he always needs a clown in the show. As for me, I think I have earned a rest. After all I have been playing all the magician parts for years now.

[*Peppino continues to peek at them from time to time.*]

BLINKIE: Then who will be the magician? And you can't stop being the magician until you can remember how to turn the strong man back into himself again.

MAGICIAN: Yes, of course, that is a little unfortunate, but as soon as I remember the spell I will attend to it.

BLINKIE: The master is still wondering where Dumbello is. He would be angry if he knew you had turned him into a chair.

MAGICIAN: Dumbello was such a nuisance. I thought he needed sitting on. [*He catches sight of Peppino peering round the curtain.*] Ah, Peppino, come out here and let us have a good look at you.

[*Peppino goes hesitatingly to centre stage and the Magician and Clown look him over with interest.*]

MAGICIAN: Well, you look quite promising, yes, quite promising.

PEPPINO: Do I? I don't know what I look like.

BLINKIE: I'm glad you are not a clown.

MAGICIAN: [*turning to the clown*] Bring the mirror, Blinkie, and let Peppino see himself.

[*Clown exits stage right.*]

MAGICIAN: [*to Peppino*] Now you will soon know what you look like. [*Clown enters stage right with property mirror which is on a stand.*] Ah, here is the mirror.

[*The clown stands the mirror on the playboard right of centre stage and facing upstage. Peppino crosses to the mirror and looks into it. He jumps back a little as though startled and then leans forward to peer into it. He then moves his head from side to side to satisfy himself that it is really he.*]

PEPPINO: [*still looking in the mirror*] Is that me? Is that what I look like?

MAGICIAN: Yes, Peppino, that is you. Don't you like you?

[*Peppino looks at the Magician and then back to the mirror as the Clown exits stage right.*]

PEPPINO: [*shaking his head*] No!

MAGICIAN: That is the way you were made, so you will have to put up with it.

[*Peppino looks at the mirror again and then at the Magician.*]

PEPPINO: I heard you say, sir, that you were the magician. Could you change my face for me?

MAGICIAN: Change your face! Why do you want to change it, and what do you want to be?

PEPPINO: [*slowly*] I think I would like to be like — like 'daughter'.

MAGICIAN: [*surprised*] Like 'daughter'! But 'daughter' is a girl — and a human being.

PEPPINO: Why can't I look like a human being?

127

MAGICIAN: But you are a puppet. You have character. Why would you want to look like a human being?

PEPPINO: 'Daughter' laughed at me when she saw me. She seemed to think I had a funny face.

MAGICIAN: That isn't anything to be ashamed of — lots of puppets have funny faces. Sometimes I wish I had a funny face. The audience likes a funny face.

PEPPINO: But I don't like to be laughed at.

MAGICIAN: You won't be so sensitive about it after you have done a few shows.

PEPPINO: I still don't want to be laughed at. Please change me to look like a human being.

MAGICIAN: All right, Peppino, if you really want me to. [*He turns and addresses the audience.*] After all, this sort of thing keeps me in practice. [*He looks around him.*] Now, where is Blinkie? He must bring my magic screen.

[*The Magician goes to each side of the stage in turn and calls 'Blinkie'. During this time Peppino is stealing glances at himself in the mirror. He then picks the mirror up and puts it down again in a similar position at stage left. He looks in it again as though moving it will have some effect on what he sees. Blinkie now enters from stage right.*]

MAGICIAN: [*seeing Blinkie*] Ah, there you are Blinkie. Will you bring me my magic screen? Peppino wants a different face.

BLINKIE: A different face! Does he know you can't remember how to turn the chair back into the strong man?

MAGICIAN: [*in stage whisper and with hand raised to lips*] Sh-h-h-h. This will give me some practice. Please bring the screen.

[*Blinkie shakes his head slowly and exits stage right.*]

MAGICIAN: [*looking at Peppino*] Now, let me see, let me see. I will give you a head like a human boy. What do you think of that?

PEPPINO: [*as Blinkie enters stage right with the screen*] That will be wonderful, then nobody will laugh at me.

BLINKIE: [*struggling with the screen*] I wouldn't be too sure if I were you.

MAGICIAN: [*ignoring the remark*] Let me think for a moment. [*He moves about the stage mumbling a jumble of spells.*] No, no, that would make you an alligator.

PEPPINO: I don't want to be an alligator; I want to be a human boy.

BLINKIE: [*who is resting the screen on the playboard at stage right*] I hope you are lucky, that's all!

128

MAGICIAN: Ah, ha, I have it! Blinkie. Hold up the screen and you, Peppino, must go behind it while I say the spell.

[*Blinkie picks up the screen and holds it up at centre stage with his back to the audience.*]

MAGICIAN: [*turning to Peppino*] You must go behind the screen now, Peppino, and come out when I have pronounced the spell.

[*Peppino goes behind the screen, but looks out once or twice, as though a bit apprehensive, while the Magician is still thinking about his spell. At this point the dog's head should be ready to put on the finger the moment Peppino's own head is removed.*]

MAGICIAN: [*suddenly*] I think I have it! Ready Peppino? [*He begins to recite a spell.*] Ippi kaki — Winni waki — count to . . . .

BLINKIE: [*interrupting*] No, no, no, that is the one you used on the strong man!

MAGICIAN: [*mildly*] Oh, is it? Then I must think again.

[*He moves around tapping his forehead as though thinking deeply. Peppino looks cautiously out from behind the screen, but ducks back again as the Magician says suddenly.*]

MAGICIAN: Now I have it! It was just the wrong way round last time.

[*He begins the spell again.*] Winni waki — ippi kaki — count to one and out you come — there!

PEPPINO: [*from behind screen*] One!

[*Peppino comes out from behind the screen to stage left. He has on the dog's head with red hair.*]

BLINKIE: [*lowering the screen a little*] What have you done now? The spell is wrong again!

[*Peppino looks in the mirror, which is still standing on the play-board at stage left, and jumps back. He then begins to bark at the reflection. The Magician looks closely at Peppino and pats him on the head.*]

MAGICIAN: It does look like it, doesn't it? [*to Peppino*] Nice dog. Now, now, now, don't worry, I must have used the wrong spell. We'll soon put it right. [*He turns to the audience.*] This is what happens when you have to stick to a script for so long — you forget your own spells.

[*The Magician turns to Peppino and pats his head again, at which Peppino growls.*]

MAGICIAN: Go behind the screen and we'll put this right.

BLINKIE: [*to the audience*] It is more likely that I will have to go for some dog biscuit.

129

[*Peppino moves towards the screen, but stops to nuzzle the clown's face. The clown backs away, still holding the screen.*]

BLINKIE: Down, down, good dog, good dog. Behind here, behind the screen. [*He holds the screen in place and Peppino obediently goes behind it.*]

MAGICIAN: If that spell wasn't right, it must be this one. [*He begins to chant.*] Hoo-do, Voo-do, what would you do? Count to three, then look at me.

[*Peppino barks three times and then comes out from the screen to stage left. This time he has the cannibal's head, with red hair. The clown lets out a frightened yell and backs away to stage right. He keeps the screen between himself and Peppino, who is executing a kind of war dance.*]

MAGICIAN: Gracious me, wrong again! [*He goes up to Peppino.*] Are you sure you want to be a human boy, Peppino? Wouldn't you like to stay as you were?

PEPPINO: [*in unintelligible language and nodding his head.*] Ha-a-a-a, gulpp, koomph, wha-a-a-a . . .

MAGICIAN: [*interrupting*] You said wha-a?

PEPPINO: Ya-ah!

MAGICIAN: Good, that will not take long. I'll soon have you looking like yourself again, but you must go behind the screen. [*He notices Blinkie still hiding behind the screen at stage right.*] Blinkie, bring the screen out here. [*Blinkie moves cautiously to centre stage with the screen. Peppino goes behind it, but he suddenly pops his head over the top. Blinkie lets out a cry and nearly drops the screen.*]

MAGICIAN: [*by now confused and a little agitated*] Let me see, let me see, where was I? Winni waki — ippi kaki [*The dog's head is poked around the screen.*] No, no, Hoo-do, Voo-do . . . [*The dog's head disappears and is replaced by the cannibal's head.*] Oh dear, why can't I get it right? Voo-do, waki . . . [*Cannibal's head reappears, quickly followed by the dog's head on the other side of the screen.*]

MAGICIAN: Oh-h, I do seem to be thoroughly confused. [*He turns to the audience.*] How am I going to make Peppino right again if I can't remember the spell? He is the master's newest puppet and he will not be pleased at all . . .

BLINKIE: [*still holding the screen*] Do hurry up and remember the spell. I can't hold the screen up much longer.

MAGICIAN: I really thought I knew it well,
How to make and break a spell;
But it seems it is beyond me.
Nothing works, not even metamorphorosomi.

[*At the word 'metamorphorosomi' Peppino comes out from behind the screen, himself again.*]

MAGICIAN: [*delighted*] Ah, that is it, METAMORPHOROSOMI [*He says this loudly. Blinkie lowers the screen and staggers with it off stage right.*]

MAGICIAN: Fancy me forgetting a simple word like that. Now, Peppino, since I remember the spell, would you like me to try again?

PEPPINO: No, no, thank you, I feel quite all right as I am. [*He looks in the mirror, still at stage left.*] I don't look so bad, do I?

MAGICIAN: Of course not. I couldn't really understand why you wanted to look like a human being instead of a puppet. Do you know that, if you looked like a human being and had to act like a puppet, you would be quite ridiculous, which is much worse than being funny. But, if you want me to, I . . .

PEPPINO: [*hurriedly interrupting*] I think I'll stay the way I am, thank you very much. I'm sure I'll get used ot it.

BLINKIE: [*entering in a state of excitement from stage right*] The strong man is the strong man again! When you shouted the spell word he changed back to himself and now he is looking for you.

MAGICIAN: [*rather hurriedly*] Well now, I really think it is time for us all to return to our hooks. The master will be back again soon and it would never do if he found us out here. Come along, come along.

[*He ushers them off to stage left as the lights dim and the curtain closes.*]

Puppetry Association and Guild Contacts

Canada   THE ONTARIO PUPPETRY ASSOCIATION
159 Frederick Street/Kitchener/Ontario

THE TORONTO GUILD OF PUPPETRY
769 Yonge Street/Toronto/Ontario

THE SOUTH WESTERN ONTARIO GUILD OF PUPPETRY
Box 238/Port Robinson/Ontario

THE EASTERN ONTARIO GUILD OF PUPPETRY
160 Billings Avenue/Ottawa/Ontario

THE PETERBOROUGH GUILD OF PUPPETRY
380 Belmont Avenue/Peterborough/Ontario

United States of America   THE PUPPETEERS OF AMERICA
7404 Tipps/Houston 23/Texas

QUAKER VILLAGE PUPPETEERS
11 Oakley Road/Upper Darby/Pennsylvania

DETROIT PUPPETEERS GUILD
450 West Kirby Avenue/Detroit/Michigan

TWIN CITY PUPPET GUILD
2077 Lincoln Avenue/St. Paul/Minnesota

PUPPET ARTS GUILD OF HOUSTON
7404 Tipps/Houston 23/Texas

LOS ANGELES COUNTY GUILD OF PUPPETRY
844 South El Molino Avenue/Pasadena 5/California

THE DETROIT INSTITUTE OF ARTS
5200 Woodward Avenue/Detroit 2/Michigan
Large permanent puppet collection; reference and research material available.

U.K.   THE BRITISH PUPPET AND MODEL THEATRE GUILD
13 Burlington Road/Chiswick/London W4/England

EDUCATIONAL PUPPETRY ASSOCIATION
239 Southampton Place/London W.C.1/England

France   SECRETAIRE ADMINISTRATIVE, SOCIETE D'HISTOIRE DU THEATRE
55 rue Saint Dominique/Paris VIIe

LE CONSERVATEUR, MUSEE HISTORIQUE DE LYON
Hotel Gadagne/14 rue Gadagne/Lyon

Brazil   NUCLEO DE ATUALIZAGAO CULTURAL
Rua Guaianazes 462/5° Andar/Sao Paulo

Germany   ARBEITSGEMEINSCHAFT FUER PUPPENSPIEL
e.v./Geschfaetsstelle/Hamburg 21/Winterhuderweg 11/Jugenheim

PROF. HARRO SIEGEL
Braunschweig/Werkakademie/Broitsemer Str.

Venezuela   QUINTA GHITEL, AVENIDA LAS PALMAS
La Florida/Caracas

Photofolio

puppets constructed

by the methods

described in this book

Hand puppets by Elizabeth Merten

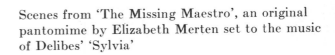

Scenes from 'The Missing Maestro', an original
pantomime by Elizabeth Merten set to the music
of Delibes' 'Sylvia'

Unless otherwise credited, all photographs
are by the author.

Hand puppets by Elizabeth Merten

Another scene from 'The Missing Maestro'

'The possapuss', a hand puppet by George Merten

Two other scenes from
'The Missing Maestro'

Hand puppets by
Elizabeth Merten

'Catch-as-catch-can'
Hand puppets with
papier-mâché heads by
Nancy Hazell

The professor, a hand puppet by George Merten

The Missing Maestro in person
A hand puppet by Elizabeth Merten

'Tango'

Hand puppets with papier-mâché heads by Nancy Hazell

Penguins, a 'formal' study in hand puppets by Nancy Hazell

Crowd scene

Puppets on the fingers of one hand by Elizabeth Merten

Slap and Dash are building up to something

Hand puppets by George Merten

Hand puppets by Brian Crabtree, Toronto

Scene from 'Punch and Judy' by Brian Crabtree

Hand puppets by
George and Elizabeth Merten

Hand and rod puppet by George and Elizabeth Merten
Note how the movement of the head gives the face varying expressions.

Honk, honk! Quack, quack!

 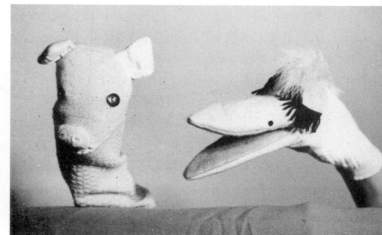

Sock puppets by Jo Gamel, Doris Aishford, Elizabeth Merten and
Marjorie Johnson

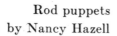 Rod puppets
by Nancy Hazell

Caterpillar Callisthenics

A rod puppet by Elizabeth Merten

Peasant boy by Jo Gamel. His bare knees are the fingers of the operator. Note the threads connecting the feet to the body to prevent the feet from becoming lost.

Look, two hands!

Finger puppets by Marjorie Johnson and Edith Sparrow

Finger puppet with hand strings by George Merten

Pastorale.

Shadow puppets by George Merten

Scene from 'The Nativity'

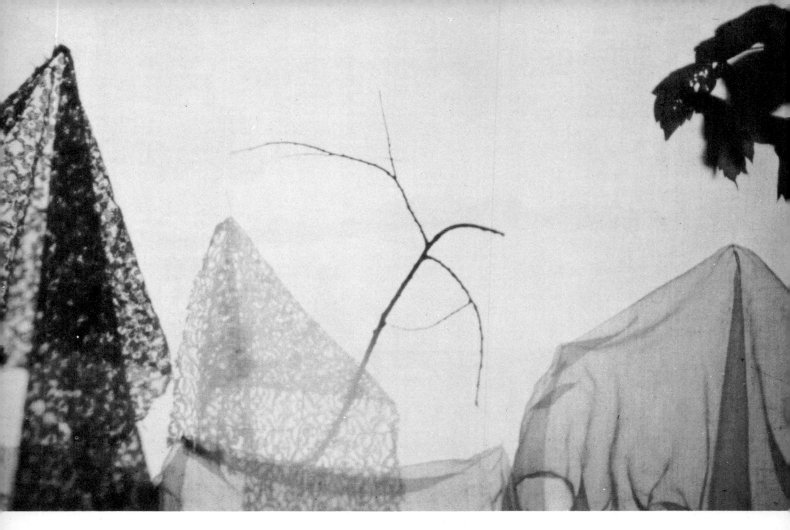

Effect created by red and blue lace, a twig, chiffon and leaves behind a shadow screen

Experimental use of coloured chiffon as background to a shadow screen